A BOOK OF GARDENS

Creative Ideas
for New Zealanders

Diana Anthony
Photographs by Gil Hanly

Foreword by Julian Matthews

David Bateman

Half title: A neatly clipped formal hedge provides a perfect foil for a floral border.

Opposite title page: Plants with dramatic foliage create a luxuriant scene in this shaded garden.

Title page: Old brick walls of mellow red create an inviting courtyard corner.

Top right: A miniature water lily in a pot is ideal for a small paved corner.

Middle right: Rhododendrons and azaleas in a spring border.

Bottom right: An imaginative grouping of pots, weathered wood and container plants.

Opposite top: An elegant outdoor entertaining room in a shaded townhouse garden.

Opposite bottom: The ruffled pink blooms of the rose 'Geisha Girl' complement the tiny pink-white single flowers of 'Ballerina'.

Published in 1995 by David Bateman Ltd,
Tarndale Grove, Albany Business Park,
North Shore City, Auckland, New Zealand

ISBN 1 86953 224 4

Front Cover: Diana Anthony's garden, 'Valley Homestead', Whangarei.

Back cover, clockwise from top left: Ayrlies, Whitford; an Auckland garden; Barnsley House, Gloucestershire; Gethsemane Gardens, Christchurch

Design by Errol McLeary
Printed in Hong Kong by Colorcraft Ltd

CONTENTS

FOREWORD

How do you make a gardening book stand out from the ever-increasing number of competing titles that crowd the bookshelves these days? It's simple. You take the most talented garden photographer in the land, combine her with someone who has an equal ability with words, and set them loose. The result is this fine book, which I know will be much loved by all who delve into its glossy pages.

How can I be so sure? Well if it can cast a spell on me, an editor who spends a good deal of his waking hours contemplating text and photographs to do with gardens, constantly running the risk of becoming jaded, then surely the magic will work for anyone who appreciates the finer things in life. And as far as I am concerned, gardens are among the finest of life's pleasures.

Gil and Diana have produced a book which is a tribute to their skills. It is also a tribute to the ability of gardeners in New Zealand who are setting a standard which is making their counterparts on the far side of the world sit up and take notice.

One reason that the standard is so high here is because of books such as this, which provide an insight into what gardeners up and down the country are achieving, plus a few of the more innovative ideas from gardeners in England and Ireland (especially in the area of potager). The books are a rich source of ideas; they spur gardeners to even greater achievements, which in turn leads to even better books.

Where will it all end, this wonderful love affair with gardening that has taken New Zealand by storm? Hopefully, like all good romances, it will go on forever, the gardens changing in a fascinating rhythm dictated by fashions, national pride and a new awareness of how much plants can enrich our lives.

One of the simplest ways of ensuring gardening is a pleasure is to grow the plants which are well suited to our conditions. This ensures the plants thrive without fuss, encouraging a relaxed attitude in the gardener. There are many examples in this book of plants suited to particular situations – from wind-lashed coastal sites where rainfall is minimal to lush and sheltered spots far inland.

There are also grand examples of gardens large and small, and each, if we use a little lateral thinking, has ideas to offer the other.

This book has something for everyone, from the armchair gardener to the dawn-to-dusk toiler. So put your feet up, enjoy, and marvel at the fact that in a few years to come the standard of gardening will be even better.

The creators of fabulous gardens at the turn of the next century will no doubt be asked what inspired them, and some will probably answer: "It was that *Book of Gardens* by Anthony and Hanly which made me realise the possibilities here." That gardener could be you.

Julian Matthews

Left: Hardy salt- and wind-tolerant trees, shrubs and phormiums create an attractive framework of shelter in this coastal garden for colourful floral plantings of marguerite daisies, mimulus and *Lavandula dentata*.

Above: Background plantings of purple- and gold-leaved maples frame this delightful small pool. The picture is made even more inviting with foreground plantings of blue grass (*Festuca ovina glauca*) and a small lavender *Brachyscome* daisy. To the right, plantings include lime-green *Alchemilla mollis,* dwarf *Scabiosa* 'Mauve Gem' and weeping grasses (*Carex* spp.). Pale grey paving stones further enhance the cool tranquil atmosphere of this most attractive water feature.

Right: The rose 'Souvenir de la Malmaison' spills sumptuous blooms over a border of pansies of apricot-pink. The eye is drawn along the inviting vista of an attractive brick walkway to fragile *Prunus* blossoms cascading onto a silvery mound of lavender. The wide hedge of dark green *Buxus* enclosing the walk emphasises the cool pale colours of the rose and other flower plantings.

COASTAL AND WINDY GARDENS

For many the spell of the sea is so hypnotic they choose to make their homes there, and, having succumbed to its magnetism, the first requisite after setting up home is to establish a garden. This is where the lesson is learned that idyllic coastal sites suffer 'sea changes' too! They can become battered by strong, salt-laden winds, and ambitious schemes and fragile plantings may suffer horribly in these climatic conditions. The old adage of choosing 'the right plant for the right place' is essential here.

Study the vegetation which is already thriving in the area. Exposed coastal locations contain a wealth of plants that have evolved over centuries in the harsh conditions created by strong, drying winds and salt spray. Such plants are the key to the success of a coastal garden. Already well suited to the environment, if given a moisture-retentive and improved soil they will thrive. The taller-growing species may be utilised to form windbreaks, providing shelter for those that are less hardy.

By planting species indigenous to coastal locations we also add to its character, preserving and enhancing it, and we are spared a good deal of frustration, heartache and expense from failed plantings!

Another bonus is that we help to preserve the birds, butterflies and insects native to the location by providing them with sustenance and shelter.

The coastal climate is not all trial, however – with the exception of the wind, it is usually one of moderation, in which the seasonal extremes of heat experienced inland are tempered and frosts are either absent or mild.

Many coastal gardens are sandy. The obvious disadvantage of thin, sandy soils is that nutrients and moisture leach away quickly. The incorporation of organic composts, mulches and watering devices, together with the all-important protection from drying winds, will do much to help establish suitable coastal plantings. There are also those that have to struggle with clay, which can be a sticky mass in winter and baked rock-hard in summer. The incorporation of organic material will help in this situation too, as will choosing the right plants.

Coastal locations where rocky conditions with scant soil prevail are equally common. It is assumed that these areas are hard to plant, but the reverse is true. There are many spectacular plants which revel in arid Mediterranean-like conditions on rocky and

Opposite: Hardy drought-tolerant species have been skilfully utilised to transform an arid windswept hilltop into a garden with exciting combinations of plant forms and foliage. In the foreground, *Scleranthus biflorus* makes velvet mounds amongst weeping grasses, *Carex flagellifera*. The broad sword-like leaves of phormiums and yuccas contrast with softer conifer forms in the background. *Astelia chathamica* 'Silver Spear' provides silvery tones and well-placed terracotta containers lend a Mediterranean flavour. Plantings have been kept low and colours restricted to soft greens and golds so that they do not detract from the magnificent ocean vista.

Tough customers are needed for plantings on this windswept hillside. In the foreground, drought-tolerant *Astelia chathamica* 'Silver Spear' is bordered by long-blooming French lavender, *Lavandula dentata*. Background plantings include low-growing foliage plants, such as coprosmas, ngaios and hebes, well suited to rugged terrain. A massed planting of silver-blue *Convolvulus mauritanicus* makes an unusual border around the edge of the lawn.

shallow soil. A choice of such shrubs might include the silver-leaved *Artemisia* species, *Senecio greyii* 'Sunshine', sea lavender *Santolina*, *Lavandula dentata* and other lavenders, rosemary, *Helichrysum* and the rock roses *Cistus*.

The seashore also offers a wealth of landscaping materials in which to arrange such plants. Sea-scoured stones and driftwood may be arranged on rocky surfaces to form stunning planting pockets and raised beds, and pathways may be made from small shells.

The provision of shelter from the wind is an essential element in a successful coastal garden. Windbreaks may be formed by the use of screens, shade cloth, fences or trellis frames, by the planting of trees and shrubs of varying height, or by a combination of both. Many coastal properties enjoy stunning ocean vistas so an important consideration in the planning of a windbreak is to allow gaps or 'windows' in the protective barriers; the object is to shut out the wind not the view!

Vegetative windbreaks filter, absorb and deflect wind energy, and experience has shown that the most effective plantings are those that modify the wind's force, rather than those forming an impenetrable barrier. When the wind is totally deflected, with perhaps a solid fence or wall, it can cause severe erosion and turbulence in adjacent areas.

Where a house creates a solid barrier against wind, plant trees and shrubs on the windward side. This helps to redirect the airflow and will have a beneficial effect on temperatures within the building. In winter the house will remain warmer inside because the flow of cold air against the walls and windows has been reduced and in summer the plantings will afford protection against the heat and drying winds.

The most effective windbreak is created by groupings of different plants, some with foliage cover to ground level, in order to direct the major force of the wind towards and over the tallest plants. To achieve this it is important to plant both the taller and the lower growing species at the same time as when foliage gaps in the maturing screen of vegetation become evident it will be much harder for new plants to establish themselves.

Another point to consider is that although solid windbreaks such as fences or walls are useful initially

Giant *Echium* spires form an amusing 'guard of honour' along the top of this garden set on a rugged coastline. Hardy, drought-tolerant plantings of day lilies, coreopsis daisies and *Lavendula dentata* – restricted in colour to blues and golds – echo a symphony of blue-grey skies, sunshine and golden beaches. An inviting place to be!

in helping plants establish and in protecting them as they grow, there is the danger that as they top the fence they will receive the full force of the wind and may snap, suffer torn roots or blow over altogether. For this reason it is preferable to construct a windbreak which will filter rather than block the wind.

Whether the windbreak is vegetative or of more solid materials, it will be most efficient at a height of approximately five metres. Relatively close planting is desirable to provide deflective foliage density, and to allow for the possibility that some plants may not survive.

Protection for young plants is essential because coastal wind carries salt and sand, and both are a problem. Salt is toxic, and when allowed to accumulate on the surface of leaves it retards the growth of buds and burns those already in leaf. This may be counteracted by regular sprayings with fresh water. Constant sand blasting has more serious effects, damaging exposed trunks and stems, especially in the case of young plants, restricting sap flow and thus plant growth. This deleterious effect may be minimised by erecting wind shelters around the plants, by wrapping them in soft cloth, or by enclosing their trunks in drums or plastic shields.

Staking young trees is also very important; the general requirement being that some degree of trunk movement be allowed. The plant should be positioned between two stakes which are set far enough apart to allow growth of a sturdy framework. The stakes should be positioned on the prevailing windward side of the plant, so that it will be blown away from them rather than against them. The ties securing the plant should be of a material such as strong cloth, rubber or plastic, which will not cause damage to the bark when the trunk moves in the wind.

There is a wide variety of trees and shrubs which will provide windbreak hedging for coastal gardens. *Abelia grandiflora* is an evergreen shrub some 1-3 m tall by a similar width, with glossy leaves toned bronze-purple in autumn and winter, when pink-red flowers also appear. *Artemisia ludoviciana* 'Silver Queen' has attractive silvery foliage and forms a dense shrub. The *Ceanothus* species, particularly the cultivar *C.* 'Blue Pacific' will grow to a height of 2-5 m and produce attractive dark blue flower heads. The common olive tree, *Olea europaea,* is an adaptable Eastern Mediterranean tree useful for screen and

The Chatham Island forget-me-not (*Myosotis hortensia*), offers unparalleled beauty of foliage and flower in a sheltered spot at the edge of a coastal garden. Massed florets of clear china-blue, with a darker eye, are borne on long stalks beneath deeply textured glossy leaves. An added bonus is that the monarch and other butterflies adore the plant's stunning blue flowers.

pleasant contrast of foliage amongst the other greens.

Some *Hebe* cultivars are well suited to coastal conditions and bloom over a long period – tall-growing *Hebe dieffenbachii* has attractive tiered foliage and can be used for windbreak planting; with an accent on sea-worthiness, the hybrids 'Miss E. Fittall', 'Hidcote' and 'Midsummer Beauty' are excellent. The evergreen shrub *Raphiolepsis indica* bears sprays of delicate, whitish-pink flowers above glossy leathery leaves, and for splendid contrast of foliage shape and form the ornamental phormiums bear upright, sword-like leaves and are hardy in coastal locations. *Coprosma* and *Pittosporum* species also offer attractive foliage contrasts.

For spectacular flowers over long periods, try *Leucospermum* and *Protea* cultivars. They thrive in well-drained soils and warm locations.

Softer effects in foreground plantings may be obtained from varieties of salt- and wind-hardy ornamental grasses such as the taller-growing *Cortaderia sellanoa* 'Gold Band' or bronze tussock, *Carex flagellifera*. Succulents, including cacti species, offer further variation, especially when the location is hot and arid.

It is even possible to have roses in a seaside garden, using the hardy *Rugosa* species. These have coarse, deeply-veined foliage and single to semi-double blooms of pink, red or white, which leave behind attractive glossy hips.

There are many flowers which will provide bright colour in the beach garden. These include the *Geranium* species, daisy bushes, *Chrysanthemum fruticans*, *Echium*, Californian poppy *Eschscholzia*, *Portulaca*, which have flowers of brilliant colours, *Alyssum*, petunias, nasturtiums, Livingstone daisies, *Mesembryanthemum*, French marigolds, *Gazania* and *Arctotis* daisies.

The taller-growing *Agapanthus* is a particularly useful flowering plant in coastal locations. In addition to its hardy nature and attractive globe flowers of blue or white, its dense, strap-like foliage grows to a height of 1.5 m, forming an effective windbreak for smaller foreground plantings.

Contrary to popular belief, the range of trees, shrubs and flowering species for coastal gardens is enormous. Provided with a little shelter all will survive to say they weathered the storm, and in your hitherto windswept, bare and sandy garden the only problem remaining will be finding space for more!

windbreak purposes. It is evergreen with grey-green leaves and will grow to between 3-6 metres. The crêpe myrtle, *Lagerstroemia indica,* makes an attractive companion plant, as its dark pink blossoms complement the silvery foliage of the olive.

The sea buckthorn, *Hippohae rhamnoides,* is often planted on sand dunes to stop them drifting. It has delightful silver foliage and slowly develops into a small, attractively gnarled tree. A most handsome evergreen shrub for coastal locations is *Griselina littoralis*, which grows fairly quickly and to a good height. The evergreen *Euonymus japonica* is a free-growing hardy shrub. It has the added bonus of coming in a golden variegated form, which makes a

Sheltered by fine coastal pohutukawa trees and wind-tolerant shrubs, this border of soft greens, golds and silvers frames the vista of sea and sky beyond. Hardy plantings include *Lavandula dentata*, marguerite daisies, *Coleonema* 'Sunset Gold', golden *Euonymus*, and clipped mounds of silver germander, *Teucrium fruticans*. Cheerful yellow arctotis daisies with silvery foliage spill onto the pathway, making a hardy border and ground cover.

Left: An exposed sandy hillside transformed into a tapestry of colour! Wonderful sea-scoured stones have been used to build up banks for this massed planting of marguerite daisies, perlargoniums, geraniums, helianthemums, pinks and nasturtiums – names which are a litany of what to plant in poor dry soils. The blue flowers of *Convolvulus mauritanicus* weave merrily through the colourful plantings, adding a cooling touch of deepest blue.

An old tree casts welcome shade over the small lawn of an urban coastal garden, and frames two appealing water views; the harbour and a swimming pool with colourful tiles. Plantings of colourful cottage garden favourites – snapdragons, petunias, verbenas, marigolds, pansies and cornflowers – combine to present an unusual combination of old floral garden style with modern landscaping design. The spiky leaves of *Astelia chathamica* 'Silver Spear' and *Cordyline* trees contrast with the cheerful sprawling of the floral plantings.

Opposite top: A gnarled pohutukawa tree stands as a sentinel at the edge of this clifftop garden, providing shelter for roses and perennials underplanted with blue catmint (*Nepeta cataria*) and furry silver *Stachys byzantina*. Clockwise from lower right, the roses are: 'Iceberg', 'English Miss', 'Mrs Finch' and tall pink 'West Coast'. The tennis court fence almost groans under the weight of the profusion of blooms borne by the rambler 'Albéric Barbier'.

Opposite bottom: Huge icy-white crystals, ancient weathered limestone, smooth rounded pebbles and slabs of granite are arranged in dramatic juxtaposition to create this exciting coastal garden. Stepping stones make an inviting pathway beside the waterway and pale water-washed pebbles form its shore. The eye is drawn across the discreet low plantings and green of the lawns to the panorama of sea and sky beyond.

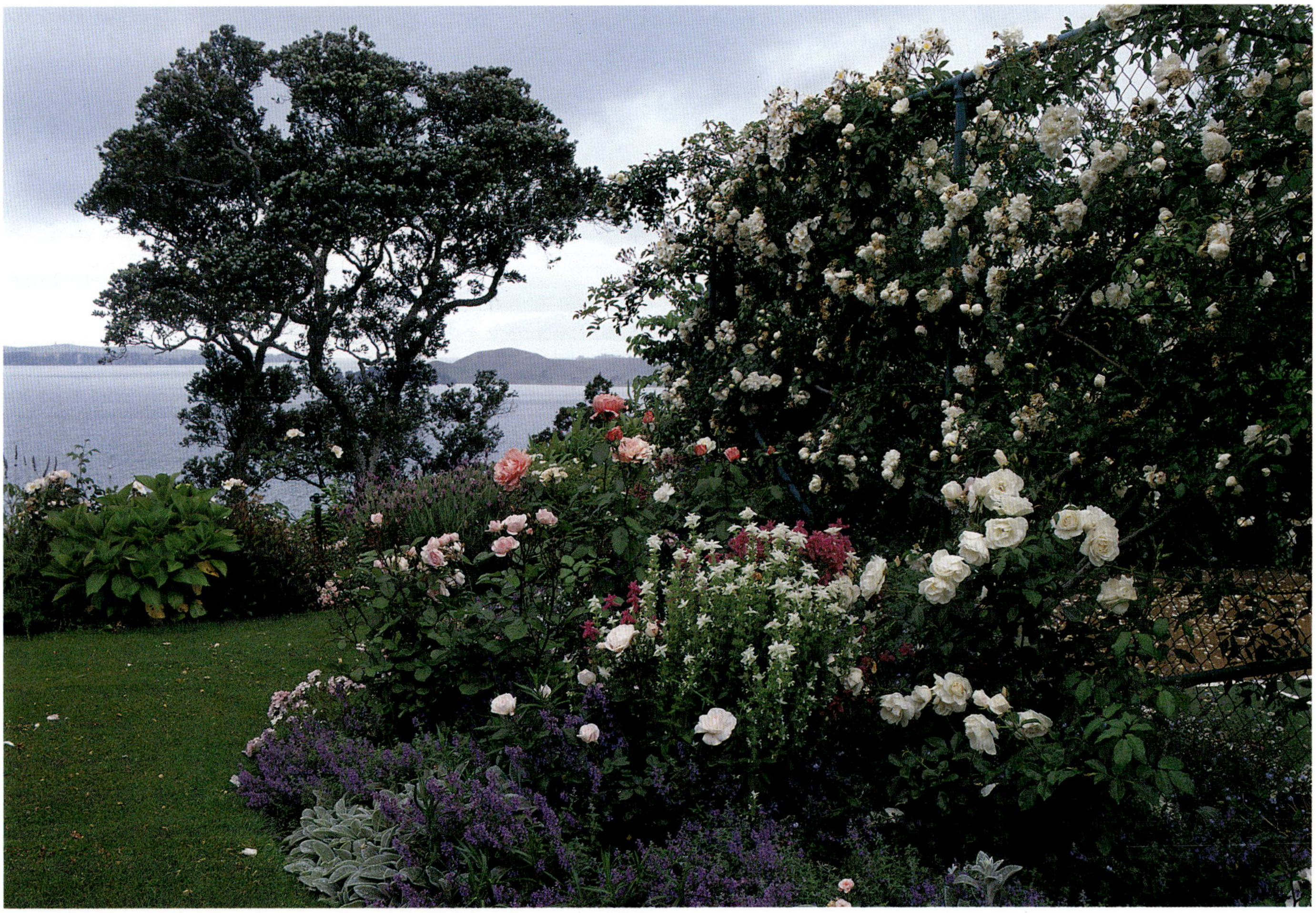

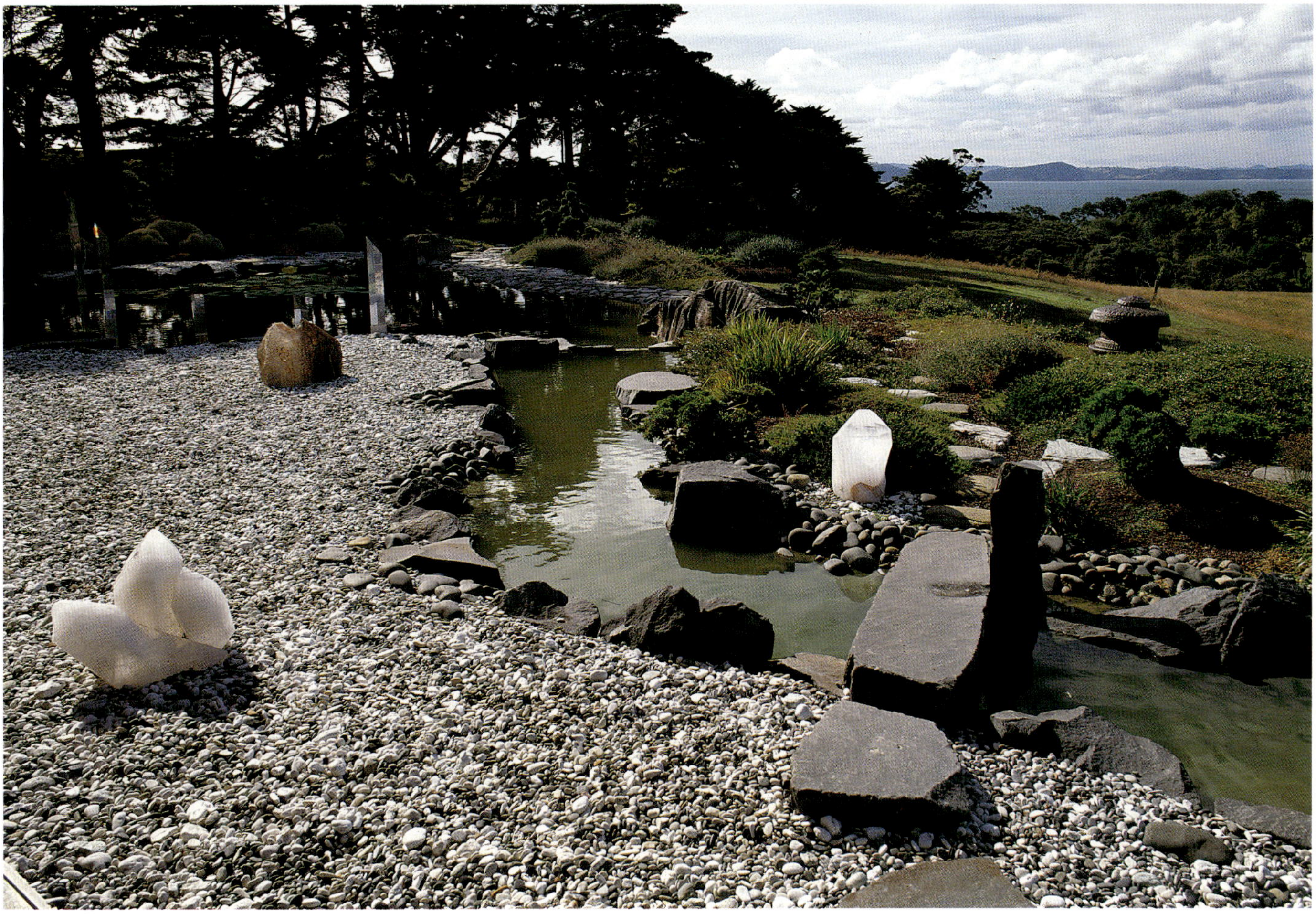

Above left: The branches of an old weathered manuka tree have obligingly grown apart to form a perfect frame for the look-out on the clifftop below. A stairway leads down through a canopy of wind-hardy, salt-tolerant trees and shrubs, to a wooden bench, which invites one to sit and admire the ocean panorama beyond.

Top right: This gay profusion of marguerite daisies, darkest blue anchusa and nerines tells its own story of what to do with a steep dry bank! In the background, the attractive foliage of a variegated *Metrosideros* and the spiky swords of a *Cordyline* make a pleasing contrast with the softer flower forms.

Above right: Half-round poles and paving stones have been used to build up planting beds on this sloping coastal section. In the foreground, massed succulents sit beneath the attractive foliage and architectural flower spikes of *Acanthus spinosus*. Background plantings include hardy blue agapanthus, a cooling colour contrast for the flame-coloured *Canna* lilies. Taller-growing *Phormium* species provide further bold foliage form.

Opposite: Sun-loving daisies shelter beneath the bright golden flowers of *Genista tinctoria*, a wind-hardy shrub suited to exposed coastal locations. A pohutukawa, along with other salt-spray and wind-tolerant trees, frames glimpses of the ocean and the borrowed landscape of a distant hill.

THE DRY GARDEN

The gardener learns many Great Truths in the course of creating and maintaining a garden, and perhaps the greatest of these is that no matter how hot, cold, wet, dry, sunny or shady a plot is, there are plants which revel in the situation, while others simply will not thrive. Despite the harshness of wind blown, mountainous, rocky or arid desert landscapes; poor, thin or sandy soils; waterlogged clay; tropical or sub-zero temperatures, such environments are the natural habitat of a wealth of attractive and hardy plants. Areas where hot, dry conditions predominate cover a good deal of the earth's surface. This need not be a case for despair but for rejoicing, because the number of plants which worship the sun far exceeds those which like to paddle or freeze!

We may choose between dramatic cacti, agaves, yuccas, phormiums and succulents; we may plant small and exquisite alpines in gravel on rocky terraces; spicy-smelling herbs which originate from Mediterranean hillsides; or flowering bulbs such as *Allium, Nerine, Romulea, Ixia, Amaryllis, Galtonia, Fritillaria* and *Sparaxis*, which do not mind sunscorched soils in the least. We may plant the hardy

tree and shrub species discussed in the Coastal Gardens chapter, which merely laugh in the face of the wind's fury; and we have an infinite diversity of hardy perennials and smaller flowering shrubs which give their all in hot, dry situations.

Originating from drought-prone deserts, shorelines, alpine herb fields or exposed rocky cliffs and scree faces, plants with silver foliage are among the most hardy and versatile species for dry garden plantings. Their silvery, grey-felted foliage is the result of a layer of fine white hairs on the leaf surface. These minimise water loss by deflecting the sun's rays and holding moisture close to the leaf face, thus keeping the tissues cool. The coastal origin of many of these plants makes them ideal subjects for dry sandy soils and where the wind factor is high.

Their blue-grey foliage is also valued for thematic gardens where colours are restricted to pale shades and subtle harmonies, and for providing a cooling foil for specimens of more brilliant and sometimes less-than-tasteful colours! Whether you are planting a beach section, an eroding clay bank, rocky terrace or windblown hill, silver plants come in a

Opposite: Striking combinations of foliage form, texture and flower colour are the components of this stunning planting on a hot, dry clay bank. From the left are: *Phormium* 'Yellow Wave', *Verbena peruviana* (brilliant red flowers in middle foreground), Mexican daisy *Erigeron karvinskianus* (bottom right), hybrid kangaroo paw *Anigozanthus* (behind and to left of small gold conifer in centre) rengarenga lily *Arthropodium cirratum* (white flowers at right) and the cream and green variegated foliage of a lacebark tree *Hoheria populnea* 'Alba variegata' (at rear).

Conifers provide form, texture and year-round interest for most gardens, and are especially suited to massed plantings on dry sloping banks such as this one. There is a shape for every situation, and bronze, silver and gold varieties provide splashes of glowing warmth on the most wretched of winter days. Their wind tolerance and ease of cultivation also makes them firm favourites for foundation plantings in any garden.

fascinating diversity of shape, form and size.

The artemisias are most attractive silver shrubs, their charm lying in the beauty of finely cut silky foliage. *Artemisia* 'Lambrook Silver' and *A. arborescens* form hardy spreading shrubs; *A. ludoviciana* provides an attractive bright silver ground cover and throws up feathery felted plumes in summer; *A.* 'Valerie Finnis' creates a dense silver white mound; and *A.* 'Faith Raven', from the mountains of Corfu, has finely cut lace-like foliage which belies its hardy nature. Most artemisias bear insignificant yellow flower heads, which are easily overlooked because of the beauty of the foliage.

The soft, elongated, furry ears of the silver plant *Stachys lanata* are excellent for interplanting in floral beds and borders where softer effects of colour and foliage are required.

Verbascum species offer an attractive change of form, growing from a thick furry rosette of basal leaves and sending up a tall flower spike of creamy-yellow or other pastel shades. *Salvia argentea* has a similarly attractive form. For sculptural effects the globe artichoke *Cynara scolymus*, the cardoon *Cynara cardunculus,* and the ornamental thistles *Eryngium, Echinops* and *Onopordum* species, are all providers of foliage ranging from deeply dissected felted silver to metallic grey-blues.

The shrub *Senecio greyii,* with its oval, downy leaves and yellow daisy-like flowers, is the ultimate 'toughie', surviving extremes of drought and salt-laden winds, and where a hardy ground cover is required, *Helichrysum argyrophyllum* roots as it spreads, finding footholds even among pebbles and rocks.

For many gardeners, gardening on a gradient is a

Looking like artwork from the brush of an impressionistic painter, massed lavender species stretch away in an enchanting lilac-blue haze. Looking at this delightful picture, one can almost smell the unique fragrance of their flowers. The popularity of lavender cultivars with bees and other beneficial insects, in addition to their beauty and scent, makes these plants favourites with almost all gardeners.

challenge. Cutting terraces, laying pathways and building retaining walls for hot dry banks, steep slopes and terraces may give head and backaches, but hardy plant materials with which to clothe them need not. Sun-loving marguerite and chrysanthemum daisy species will thrive in such areas – as will Cape daisies, the dimorphothecas. The latter form a thick mat of attractive green foliage smothered with flowers of pink, wine, purple-mauve or creamy yellow. There is an attractive hybrid called 'Silver Sparkle', with cream and green variegated foliage. The *Gazania, Arctotis* and *Coreopsis* daisies are also members of this hardy sun-loving group.

Mesembryanthemum, or ice plant, species provide brilliant colour, and nasturtiums will scramble over the most inhospitable of terrains. They now come in a range of attractive hybrids such 'Whirly Bird',

offering rich shades of gold, russet-red and bronze. Both species need arid conditions to flower well – one should not quarrel with such attributes! *Convolvulus mauritanicus* – no relation of the dreaded invasive species – offers cool blue chalice flowers amongst brighter blooms, as do the drought-tolerant shrubs *Ceanothus, Hebe* and *Plumbago.*

Among other smaller shrubs to enhance hot dry slopes, *Cistus* (rock rose), with their prolific tissue-paper flowers, are tried and tested. *Cistus corbariensus* is extremely hardy and has yellow-centred flowers above grey-green foliage; *C. ladaniferus* has white flowers with a fascinating eye dotted black; *C.* 'Silver Pink' is one of the prettiest hybrids; and *C.* 'Bennett's White' is the aristocrat of the species, with magnificent white silky flowers and a boss of golden stamens.

There is a touch of humour about this dramatic garden with its imaginative juxtaposition of plant forms and colours. The spiky swords of silvery-green *Agave attenuata* and the flower towers of *Echium pininana* are illuminated from behind by the brilliant shrimp-pink spring foliage of the toon tree *Cedrela sinensis*. In the left foreground, silver-blue *Echeveria elegans* and spiny cacti are planted near the bushy succulent *Crassula*.

Geraniums and pelargoniums are favourite candidates for sun-drenched gardens, offering a wide range of petal colour and scented leaves, and no self-respecting baked clay bank would be without generous plantings of *Agapanthus,* which grow in the most adverse conditions. When not in flower its glossy strap-like foliage still provides clumps of attractive stabilising ground cover.

For architectural effect and winter colour among the flower forms in dry soils, use weeping grasses, dwarf bamboos, massed succulents or cacti amongst rocks and pebbles to create contrast of shape, texture and form.

For year-round interest, the conifer species come in sizes and shapes for all dry garden situations, giving pleasing colours through many greens, golds,

bronzes and blues. They are also surprisingly wind hardy in exposed or coastal areas. Shrubs with coloured, evergreen and variegated foliage for year-round interest might include those discussed in the chapter on foliage gardens. Another provider of rich colour is the drought-tolerant small shrub *Nandina domestica* 'Pygmaea', which bears slender leaves of crimson, gold and plum throughout the seasons.

Many herbs love dry conditions and give attractive foliage contrast, form and scent. Favourite species include the lavenders, rosemary, oregano, the thymes, sages, santolina, fennel, marjoram and yarrow.

In areas where thin soil and stony ground predominate, many gardeners look to rock gardens and the alpine species. These hardiest of small plants survive inhospitable conditions such as thin gritty soils, searing winds, sharp drainage, long hot summers and, in some cases, snow cover during part of the year. Many adapt to such hostile situations by forming a compact, ground-hugging, wind-defying form which makes them suitable for growing in rockeries and other small areas.

In gardens which are both rocky and sloping, alpines may be planted in a scree bed stabilised by outcrops of larger stones, or tucked into pockets in retaining walls. Other plants suitable for alpine and rock gardens are dwarf species of *Dianthus, Aubrietia, Campanula, Saxifraga, Sempervivium, Lewisia, Phlox, Gentian* and edelweiss.

Year-round interest can be maintained with dwarf rhododendrons, azaleas, conifers and *Erica* species (heathers). There is also a wide range of miniature bulbs and corms which provide carpets of colour over long periods.

Last but not least for gardens where water is a problem is the provision of the all-important shade trees. Those which will tolerate dry conditions are more common than is supposed and might include *Magnolia grandiflora, Albizia, Cedrela sinensis, Hymenosporum, Jacaranda,* taller conifers and evergreens, silver-leaved cultivars, *Betula* and *Ulmus* species.

Lack of rainfall can be compensated for to a certain degree by the installation of irrigation systems which provide a gentle supply of water over long periods and by heavy mulching. If the garden situation does not allow these options, there is a wealth of plants which revel in sun-baked roots.

Above: Gardening on the rocks! Heat-loving plants wander with delightful informality across the top of this dry hillside. An eye-catching massed planting of rengarenga lilies (*Arthropodium cirratum*) in full flower makes a dramatic feature in the bed right of centre.

Left: The moss *Scleranthus biflorus* forms lime-green velvety mounds amongst large rocks, their surfaces attractively patterned with lichens. In the background, sun-loving marguerite daisies create a cheerful scene behind a hedge of drought-tolerant rosemary.

This garden situation presents the dual challenge of severe wind and dry soil conditions.
The gardener has risen admirably to the challenge, planting heat-loving euphorbias, spiky blue
echiums, silver-grey artemisias and red penstemons. The attractive grass with lime-green tassels is
Chionochloa flavicans, and the white flower heads of an *Achillea* hybrid highlight the centre of
the border. Tree and shrub plantings have been restricted to lower growing species which can
cope with the high winds.

Opposite top: The pale cool plantings of blue and silver bordering the steps imparts an ambience
of quiet serenity in a rugged environment. The staircase of grey weathered sleepers invites one to
climb to the top and look down on the restful plantings. Paired upright shrubs and stately blue
irises at the base of the steps make a pleasing architectural statement, and the bark of the silver
birch blends beautifully with the grey-leaved plantings. The quiet colours harmonise with the
silver-blue tones of the sky.

Opposite bottom: Many alpines have adapted themselves to severe winds by having a low growth
habit. In this attractive garden they make a colourful embroidered carpet on gravelly soil, amongst
rocks encrusted with lichens.

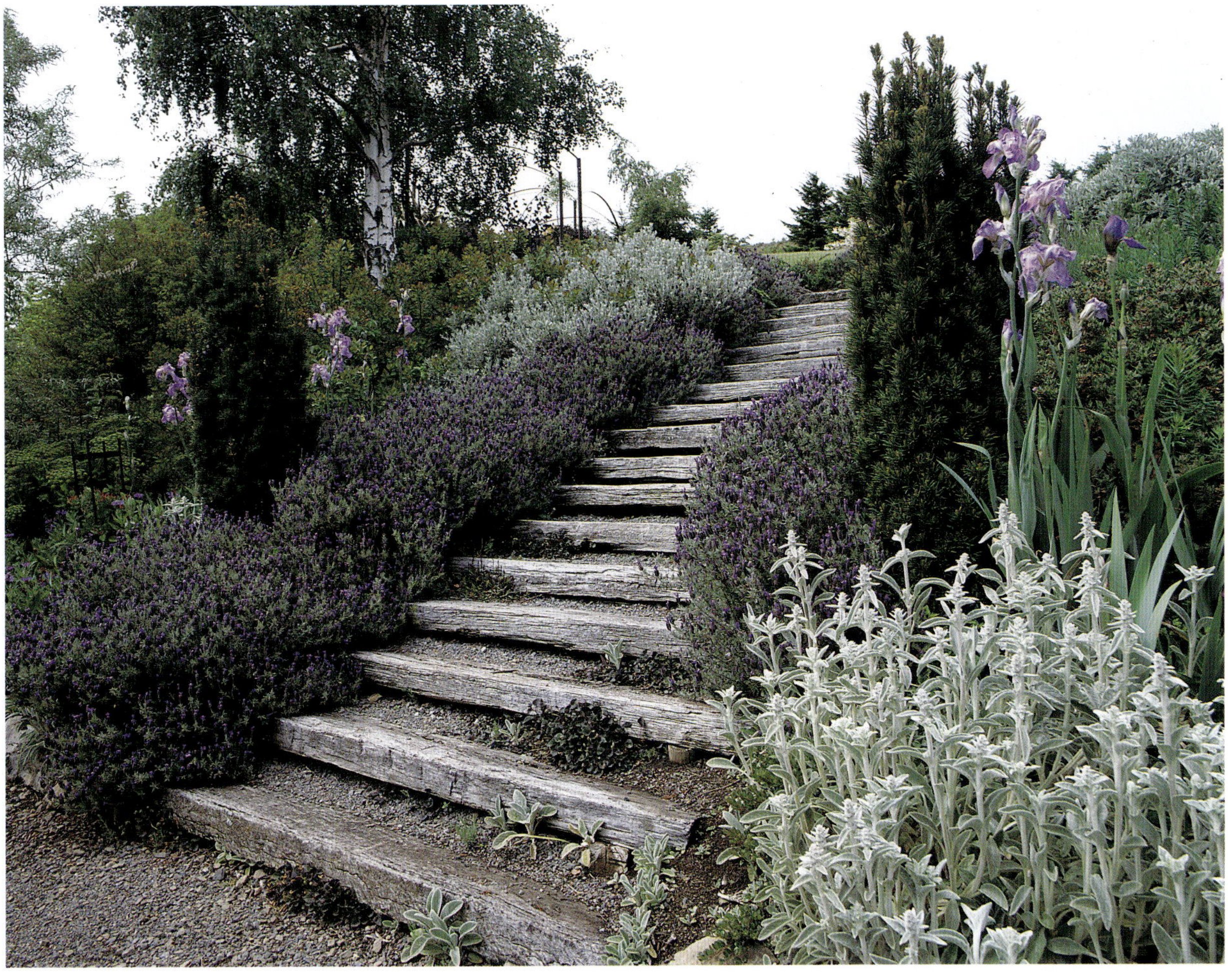

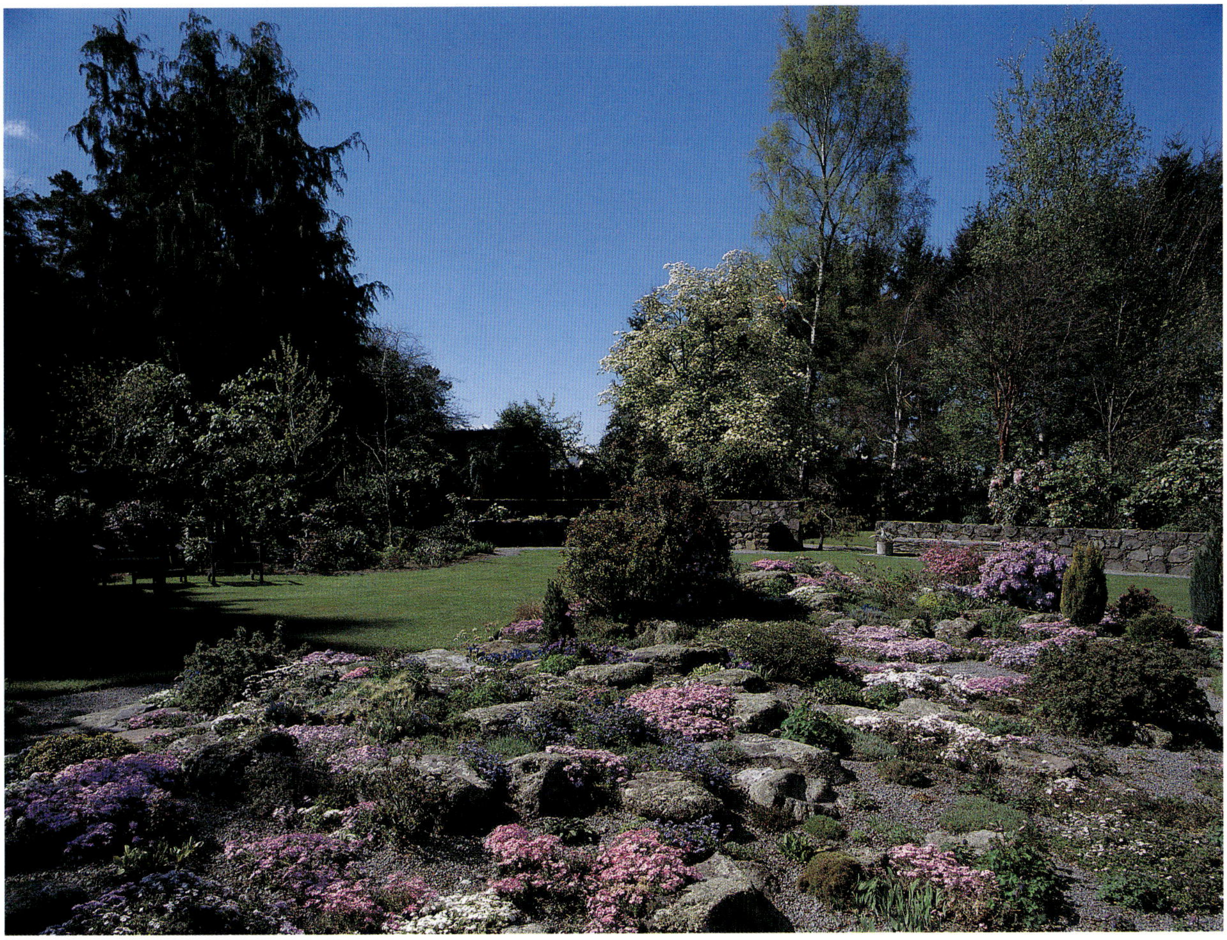

A fascinating piece of geometrical landscaping emerges from this new and developing dry garden area. The small circular pool in the centre of the spokes will make a dramatic juxtaposition with silver-leaved sun-loving plants. Clumps of *Artemisia* 'Valerie Finnis' border the entrance to the circle, and plants to the left are: catmint *Nepeta fassenii*; the shrub *Senecio greyii*; *Cynara scolymus* (globe artichoke), with huge felted leaves of silver; and silver germander, *Teucrium fruticans*. Plantings on the right of the weathered wooden bench include globe artichokes, cerise *Lychnis coronaria* and furry *Stachys lanata*.

Opposite top left: Some like it hot! This steep dry bank has been transformed into a pot-pourri of blue and yellow sun-worshipping plants. Beneath the tree silhouetted against a heat-filled sky, *Echium fastuosum* throws up bee-encrusted blue flower spires through a mass of golden daisy-like blooms.

Opposite top right: How inviting this pathway of grey gravel looks meandering through drought-resistant silver, grey and white plantings, drawing the eye through the archway to the sky beyond. One longs to step into the picture and sit on the white seat which emphasises the cool freshness of the plantings. The weeping silver pear, *Pyrus sacilifolia* 'Pendula', shades the bench, and the attractive silky white flowers in the foreground are those of godetia. The left side of this tempting pathway is bordered by white pansies, marguerite daisies and white hydrangeas.

Opposite bottom left: An interesting selection of succulents, together with furry *Stachys lanata*, are massed amongst huge old tree roots at the foot of a dry clay bank. The attractive weeping tree in the centre of the picture is the Chinese parasol tree, *Japonica sophora* 'Pendula'. *Astelia chathamica* 'Silver Spear', yuccas and variegated phormiums thrive on the arid slope, and the gold fronds of a weeping conifer provide a little shade in an otherwise hot, dry area.

Opposite bottom right: Yellow *Alyssum saxatile*, *Helianthemum* 'Sunset Pink' and prostrate rosemary all love dry conditions, and here tumble from the top of a stone wall creating a pleasing composition of bold colour.

Following pages: A garden in a river bed: the occupant of this old cottage, which once stood near a river, has created a highly individual garden of enchanting simplicity. The plants meander softly through water-scoured pebbles, suggesting the gentle flow of water. Nearer the cottage, plants tolerating dry conditions include (left) a mound of silver germander, *Teucrium fruticans*, fronted by a dark purple *Salvia officinalis*; (centre) variegated *Euonymus* and *Coleonema* 'Sunset Gold' provide warm foliage colourings; and (foreground) the small pink-tipped daisy *Erigeron karvinskianus* and marguerite daisies billow through the stones with delightful freedom.

GARDENS IN THE SHADE

Shade should be viewed not so much as a problem, but an opportunity – it is a positive asset; an integral and essential component of the overall design requirement of every garden. In Victorian and Edwardian days the secluded and often gloomy shrubbery provided just the right amount of shade and protection for the genteel dalliance of formally dressed ladies and gentlemen. Restrictive layers of clothing and a milk-white skin meant parasols could only be lowered beneath trees, and decorous meals were taken on lawns shaded by their canopy.

Today, alfresco meals enjoyed by the side of a swimming pool must be taken beneath contrived shade, as protection against skin cancer. For many gardeners it is the provision of this shelter, rather than its utilisation once acquired, which presents a problem. A garden without shade is a hot and tiring place. To be comfortable and successful, gardens require the juxtaposition of brilliant sunlight enlivened by the movements in dappled shade.

Areas of dim light in the garden are usually interpreted in four ways: dense shade, semi-shade, dry shade and wet shade.

Dense shade may be caused by mature trees with spreading branches or by buildings. In hotter climates this form of permanent dense shade is provided by pergolas, deep verandahs or corridors planted with heavy climbers. Soil conditions in deep shade are often heavy and wet, and require plantings with species which thrive in such locations.

Areas of semi or dappled shade may receive sunlight for only part of the day, or be lightly shadowed by overhanging vegetation or buildings. This type of shade is perhaps the most pleasant of all, as the soft light will support an immense variety of plant life. Many of the world's most famous rhododendron, azalea and camellia gardens are situated in light woodland enjoying dappled shade, and the soil in these areas is rich and fertile with a wealth of leaf mould and natural organic matter.

Dry shade situations occur where soil moisture is depleted by the roots of trees and darkened by their canopy, or where rain cannot reach under the eaves of buildings.

Although the density of the shade may vary, almost all shaded locations provide the medium for

Opposite: Soil beneath the shade of eaves and alongside narrow pathways often presents extremes – too dry or too damp. In this case, the gardener has utilised species adaptable to either condition, creating an inviting pathway bordered by lush green foliage. Variegated ivies, silver streaked *Lamium* and ferns are used as ground cover. Taller plantings include shade-loving fuchsias and fairy bamboo, *Bambusa* 'Gracilis'. The huge glossy leaves of an *Aroid* hybrid provide striking foliage contrast amongst the other plantings.

A sheltered path beneath the trees invites one to follow the timbered walkway across a large pool. The eye is drawn to the dramatic architectural foliage of *Gunnera manicata*, and to the fascinating water sculptures on the left. Subdued colour plantings enhance the many varying shades of green, and create the atmosphere of a shaded and tranquil woodland glade.

the creation of strong focal points and features. To step from harsh sunlight into the semi-shade of a woodland glade, or to find a seat in a shadowed arbour, is a refreshing and welcome experience. The tantalising glimpse of a piece of pale statuary or of a small tranquil pool amidst luxuriant dark green foliage extends a tempting invitation. The dim cool of a shadehouse filled with interesting plants can also provide a pleasing feature.

Shadowed sites behind inner-city dwellings may be transformed into delightful walled or courtyard gardens. Planted with a small shade tree and perennials which thrive in low light, such as *Clivia, Campanula, Impatiens, Acanthus* and *Bergenias,* such locations provide a cool green haven.

A sheltered corner may lend itself to a thematic approach, such as an oriental garden planted with maples. The exquisite lacy foliage of these small trees

requires protection from hot sunlight and wind and they are well suited to such an area. Attractive stones and boulders will amass soft mosses and lichens in the half light, and the incorporation of a small water feature or pool completes the design.

A similarly pleasing approach might be the planting of shade-tolerant bulbs and wild flowers to create a simple woodland effect. A subtropical or 'jungly' flavour might be interpreted by the planting of shade-loving plants with lush, bold foliage, together with lusty climbers bearing bright flowers. Many plants have adapted to shade by developing larger leaves, making for strong planting styles.

Where dense shade prevails, the object will be to introduce colour and relief with plants bearing bright flowers and foliage offering as wide a variety of leaf shape, form and texture as possible. The many species of the shade-loving *Hydrangea macrophylla*,

Massed blooms of the enchanting candelabra primulas, which carry their blooms in tiers, create a symphony of gentle colour in a damp area shaded by mature trees. The bold variegated foliage of *Hosta* hybrids provides a dramatic contrast to the delicacy of the flowers.

some of which have variegated foliage and flowers of mauve, blue, pink and white, would be a good choice. *Hypericum* bears masses of bright gold flowers during summer through autumn, and drifts of flowers such as *Impatiens* and *Pachysandrus,* which bears bright scarlet flowers, will naturalise to form colourful carpets over long periods.

Some areas of dense shade are also wet, and thus dictate a bog or water garden effect. Nowhere does foliage take on a more dramatic role than near water. There is a wealth of plant material and flowers which revel in wet feet and dim light, and many of those discussed in the section on water gardens would be suitable for such a location. The *Hosta* species offers a huge range of foliage effects; silver, gold and variegated cream-and-green-splashed deeply textured leaves of many sizes. All bear delightful flowers of white, blue or mauve. For drama, the giant leaves of

Gunnera manicata or *Rheum palmatum* 'Atrosanguineum' are unrivalled, and for softer effects damp- and shade-loving ferns offer a pleasant contrast.

Floral colour in damp shade may be provided by plantings of Iris; *Primula* species, such as *P. japonica* or *P. florindae,* which has flowers like giant cowslips; the monkey musk *Mimulus luteus,* with attractive, serrated leaves and flowers of gold, dark red or mahogany; *Caltha palustris,* the marsh marigold, which lightens shade with large, buttercup-like flowers of burnished gold; and astilbes, with their filmy spires of crimson, pink or white above glistening dark fern-like foliage.

Dry shade is more difficult to utilise than damp shade. Occurring most often under the shadow of dense tree plantings or overhanging buildings, this is often a situation of permanent shade, since it is not subject to varying degrees of light or seasonal changes. These areas too often become notoriously dry, barren and uninviting unless carefully planned and planted. Building up and enrichment of the soil, automatic irrigation systems and the incorporation of water retentive 'Liquid Rain' crystals at the base of planting holes will all help to sustain plant life in such depleted locations.

If the area is large, an alternative to hard-won beds and plantings might be to utilise it as a shady, paved outdoor living area. Overhanging trees may have their lower branches judiciously pruned to let in more light and sunshine and densely foliaged trees and shrubs may be thinned to create dappled light. Be careful to retain the natural shape of the plant when pruning. Colour and variety in leaf texture and form may be provided by groupings of plants in containers.

Ground cover plants for dry shade could include ivy, *Hedera helix,* which has an attractive variegated leaf; the aluminium plant (*Pilea* species); *Lamium galeobdolon* or *L. maculatum* 'roseum'. The former has light green variegated foliage and yellow flowers and the latter pale green leaves splashed with pink and pink flowers. These plants can become invasive in good soils, but are invaluable for locations where impoverished dry soil and dense shade predominate.

Aucuba japonica 'Variegatum' is a shrub which tolerates such conditions and gives attractive gold and green speckled foliage. *Cornus canadensis,* a species of dogwood with light green foliage that bears white flowers in summer, also enjoys deep shade.

Flowering plants which will bring colour into inhospitable situations do exist! They include *Anemone nemorosa,* the pink-white wood anemone; *Cyclamen* species; foxgloves; bluebells; bleeding heart *Dicentra eximia; Helleborus* varieties; and lilac-purple or white honesty flowers, *Lunaria,* followed by attractive coin-like silver seed pods.

Another common location of shade is that formed by narrow pathways or corridors between houses and fences. These places can look dark and uninviting. The innovative gardener turns such a situation to advantage by providing moisture if necessary and planting a lush fernery, ground covers and exciting shade-tolerant climbers.

These could include *Actinidia,* a vigorous deciduous climber with fragrant green-white flowers and foliage that is tinged with pink; *Akebia quinata,* a deciduous climber with blue-green foliage and deep purple flowers in spring; *Hardenbergia comptoniana,* an evergreen that spreads quickly and bears masses of lavender blue flowers in early summer; the climber *Hibbertia scandens,* with glossy deep green foliage and yellow flowers all summer (it will also tolerate dry conditions); Virginia creeper, *Parthenocissus quinquefolia,* will quickly clothe shaded walls and has brilliant autumn foliage. Jasmine, honeysuckle and wisteria species will also cope with, and bring colour and bloom to, shaded locations.

Landscape techniques and alternatives for shady gardens are exciting and varied. The thematic approaches discussed in this section would suit a wide range of climatic conditions, and be equally attractive in city or rural locations. The philosophy is that if you have a shaded situation and can't beat it, turn it into a focal point.

A pair of stunning pottery vases and an attractively paved curving path combine to create a design of bold simplicity, making this small garden an inviting place to be. Plantings are restricted to a soft and restful harmony of pinks and greens.

Above: A *Hosta* hybrid with bold, deeply textured leaves dominates other shade-loving plantings. Deep blue aquilegias and a flame-coloured azalea add complementary colour to this garden where light is restricted.

Left: An attractive bench of natural wood and lush foliage create an oasis of green beneath the shade of surrounding trees. Plants tolerant of low light situations include *Hosta* cultivars, the Japanese wind anemone *Anemone hupenhensis* and *Rhododendron* species. The purple-black leaves of *Prunus nigra* makes pleasing contrast with the rich green of the foliage in the beds beneath.

Opposite top left: Sunlight filtering through the canopy of overhead trees illuminates the rich golden-yellow of rhododendrons and azaleas, creating a picture of warmth despite the garden area being subject to fairly dense shade.

Opposite top right: Many gardeners experience the problem of trying to establish plantings in soil robbed of nutrients and moisture at the foot of mature trees. The owner of this garden has coped with these conditions by transforming an otherwise unattractive area into a spring carpet of forget-me-nots and cineraria flowers. In other seasons, bulbs tolerating low light and hardy ground covers could be planted to maintain interest.

Opposite bottom left: The fact that areas of dense shade and dry soil conditions need not be barren and unattractive is beautifully demonstrated by this stunning planting of massed clivias. Each stalk carries generous clusters of orange flowers with a golden throat, and when not in bloom the plant's glossy, dark green, strap-like leaves combine to make a handsome clumping ground cover.

Opposite bottom right: Situated beneath a canopy of trees, this courtyard garden offers an intimate green retreat. The eye is drawn towards the pair of earthenware pots, which create a strong focal point in front of a flame-coloured rhododendron. In the right foreground, the shade-loving dwarf maple, *Acer dissectum* 'Viridis' weeps lace-like foliage, and further right sunlight illuminates the golden foliage of a *Gleditsia* tree.

Top right: Repeated plantings of the handsome green-and-cream-splashed leaves of *Hosta fortunei* 'Alba-Picta' steal the scene at the front of a rhododendron border, thriving where low light conditions prevail.

Bottom right: Ferns throw up luxuriant fronds in the moist soil of a border well shaded by overhanging trees. A bird bath tucked into their lacey foliage makes an attractive feature, and lavender rhododendron flowers provide gentle colour amongst restful green plantings.

Top left: Plants requiring semi-shaded conditions thrive beneath the attractive panelled roof of a trellised shade house. Dark green painted woodwork harmonises beautifully with the foliage colours of the plantings.

Centre left: An attractive assortment of plantings shows that narrow, shaded pathways alongside houses need not be problem areas. A bed of ferns and the weeping sword-like leaves of *Phormium* 'Yellow Wave' highlight the border opposite. A background planting of purple-black foliage makes an effective contrast with that of a young kauri, a young totara and pink-flowered leptospermums. Weathered railway sleepers make an attractive edging.

Bottom left: Vivid magenta spires create a strong focal point and a sharp contrast with restful greens at the edge of this pleasant shaded pathway.

Opposite: Drama of foliage texture and form is the essential element of the luxurious plantings alongside this inviting timbered walkway. In the background, the lancewood *Pseudopanax crassifolium* resembles a half-closed umbrella with very narrow, serrated, downward-drooping leaves. Other plant species revelling in this situation of damp shade include *Gunnera manicata*, ferns, hostas and astilbes.

SUBTROPICAL AND EXOTIC GARDENS

The subtropical or exotic garden conjures up exciting images of lush foliage, flamboyant colour, plants of bold structure, shadowed canopies of tree ferns and palms, tangled climbers, breath-taking bromeliads, orchids and other opulent flowers. It is filled with warmth and is dramatic in style. In warm, moist locations the luxuriance of its rich green depths has all the sensuous beauty and mystery of a South Seas paradise. The humidity lends itself to the creation of secret pools or bold water gardens where flowers of brilliant colour and plants with striking foliage are clumped around the margins, reflecting mirror images into the water. Overhead, rampant vines and climbers scramble to the sunlight and let fall flashy blossoms.

The subtropical garden is a dynamic year-round garden because growth and bloom are sustained by temperate conditions, and are not subject to seasonal die-back. The exotic garden requires less mainten- ance, and is far less demanding in the planting, feed- ing and pruning than the traditional floral garden. Its style is less formal and emulates the original rain forest or semi-desert landscape habitat of its plants.

In the drier extremes of hot and arid locations, the subtropical or exotic garden offers the drama of a desert landscape, punctuated with fleshy succulents and the spiked silhouettes of cacti of many forms. There are spectacular agaves, aloes and plants with fantastic sword-like foliage and strange flowers. The damp, mossy and ferny floor of the warm, wet sub- tropical garden is replaced with rocks, sun-baked pebbles, shingle or burning sand.

The concept of an exotic garden is exciting in its versatility because it may be created in large or small places, in containers, around decking, patios and verandahs – in any geographical location which enjoys year-round warmth and winters free from frost. For the lush rainforest atmosphere, sufficient

Opposite: Sharp geometric landscaping and the drama of plant form are the essential factors in this striking subtropical urban garden. In the foreground, a low-growing *Sedum* and the bushy green-gold succulent *Crassula* are strategically placed between huge boulders. The upright spears of *Sanseveria* (centre) create further bold foliage form. Silvery succulents are used as bedding plants under sculptural dragon trees (*Dracaena draco*), which dominate the skyline and reflect mirror images in the waterway. Plantings employed in this garden are well suited to subtropical areas where arid conditions prevail.

The clustered flowers of three subtropical vireya rhododendrons provide glowing pools of colour amongst the bold dark foliage of other plantings. The *Rhododendron* cultivars are yellow-throated pink 'Kisses', orange 'Golden Charm' and 'Pink Delight'. Beneath mossed rocks clumps of the silver-banded bromeliad *Aechmea fasciata* offer further variety of sculptured foliage form.

rainfall is necessary, but the overall theme of the garden is concerned less with climate than with approach and style.

The basic design for the exotic garden must incorporate shade, which both plants and humans need. A vegetative canopy may be provided by pergolas, trellis frames and terraces, over which dense coverings of evergreen climbers have been planted. Blinds of canvas, bamboo, rattan or giant umbrellas may be utilised to screen outdoor living and eating areas.

The aim in the planting design is for a good balance at different levels between plants with extravagant foliage and flowers of riotous colour. Plants in the subtropical garden do not whisper, they make loud statements! Although brilliant flower colour sets an exotic mood, it is the form and texture of the other plantings which enhance their brilliance and provide the essential backdrop.

Tall-growing tree ferns will give vertical structure above lower growing ferns, aroids, shrubs and ground coverings. Vertical plantings play an essential part in the creation of a vegetative canopy. Climbers such as *Bougainvillea spectablis* and *B. glabra* offer singing colours of magenta, orange, yellow and white.

Pyrostegia venusta bears massed clusters of burnt orange tubular flowers which provide sensational displays over a long period. The sky-blue flowers of the climber *Thunbergia grandifolia* make an excellent foil and cool the exuberant colour of *Pyrostegia*.

The trumpet vine, *Campsis radicans,* and the passionflower vine, *Passiflora caerulea,* are quick-growing, will provide exotic atmosphere and have the added virtue of being hardy in cooler temperate locations. The former has huge orange-apricot flowers and the latter exquisite purple-and-green-flushed-white flowers followed by passionfruit. Gardeners have been known to design an exotic garden just so they might grow a passionflower vine!

Hanging containers with trailing ferns, orchids or bromeliads also play an important part in adding to overhead plantings.

Container plantings are particularly useful in the exotic garden. The flowers of many subtropicals are extravagant but short-lived, so flowers such as *Canna* and *Gloriosa* lilies, orchids, *Aphelandra,* bougainvilleas or epiphytic bromeliads grown in containers may be moved to centre stage when they are at their most eye-catching, adding theatrical colour combinations of electrifying oranges, reds, yellows and pinks. Plants with enormous glossy foliage of rich dark green such as 'Giant's Ears', *Alocasia macrorrhiza,* or climbing philodendrons provide the perfect foil to the flowers' flashy colour.

Plantings of varied species of taller-growing ferns are an essential component of the subtropical garden. They provide filtered shade and delicacy of frond and spathe in contrast to the architectural form of the lower, bolder plants. Among the larger varieties come *Cyathea australis* and *C. arborea,* the West Indian tree fern. The former is an adaptable undemanding specimen, often grown in containers for smaller gardens, and is relatively cold-hardy in cooler climates. The latter can reach a height of seven metres and has fronds of a delicate light yellow-green. Of the *Dicksonia* fern species, *D. antarctica* is grown worldwide because it prefers cool temperate climates rather than true hot subtropical conditions.

It would be difficult to imagine an exotic garden without the graceful arching fronds of palm trees.

Growing from a tree fern log, the big bromeliad *Aechmea pineliana* throws up glowing leaves beneath a *Tetrapanax* (rice paper tree). Both create exciting reflections in the pool, and hot orange-red crucifix orchids (left) cluster under drooping palm fronds, adding to the exotic ambience of the garden.

Like tree ferns, they have the added virtue of being suitable container subjects for small gardens or less temperate climates. The Kentia palm, *Howea forsteriana,* is particularly useful for this purpose, and has fine spine-tipped fronds and a well-ringed straight trunk.

Butia capitata is an easy palm to grow; it is tolerant of both cool temperatures or full sun and a wide range of soils. The Japanese sago palm, *Cycas revoluta,* is favoured for its lower growth habit and architectural form. It has a bold central coronet above stiff dense fronds and an attractive thick trunk. This versatile cycad is widely grown because it suits many locations, being tolerant of sun, wind and drought.

The soft arching fronds of *Phoenix roeblinii,* the dwarf date palm, look stunning overhanging water gardens and the European fan palm, *Chamaerops humilis,* is well suited to smaller gardens. For a taller grower the fan or windmill palm, *Trachycarpus fortunei,* is favoured for the spread of its broad fronds. The

nikau palm, *Rhopalostylis sapida,* is also an attractive specimen which tolerates less temperate climates.

At ground level there is a wealth of smaller ferns suitable for ground cover and containers. Perfect partners for their feathery softness are the epiphytic bromeliads which have been called 'designer plants'. This reputation is well deserved for they are plants of fascinating form, giving striking colour at ground level. They need no soil as their natural habitat is on trees, stumps of wood or rocks. They use their roots for anchorage rather than feeding, taking moisture and nutrients (such as insects and their eggs) from the air into their colourful central rosette.

The lustrous strap-like leaves of bromeliads come in varying sizes and lengths which may blend three or four colours into stunning combinations. Some have patterns, ranging from stripes and spots to dapplings and bandings, and their hearts are pools of fire. No seeding, pricking out or replanting is necessary with bromeliads – they reproduce freely by

The subtropical garden is a garden of bold foliage and dramatic form – one almost expects to look over the fence of this sun-drenched courtyard and see a heat haze shimmering over a distant desert! Attractively shaped terracotta pots contain drought-tolerant plants of weird and wonderful shapes. *Aloe plicatilis*, looking like a giant bonsai, grows in the square pot; to its left stands a spiky *Euphorbia*, and behind is the variegated *Cordyline* 'Albertii'. The small tufted plant to the right of the empty pot is *Echinocactus grusonii* and the squat spiny cactus is an *Astrophytum* hybrid.

sending out new plants or 'pups'. They are to the exotic garden what a perennial is to the traditional one!

Flowers providing softer form and colour in the underplanting of the subtropical garden include *Impatiens,* bergenias, clivias, *Calathea, Stromanthe,* begonias, aphelandras and the Japanese anemone. The *Gloriosa* lily, *G.* 'Rothschildiana', has dramatic reflexing fluted petals of flaring yellow and red over stiffly prominent stamens, and it has a particularly exotic appeal.

The 'bird of paradise' plant, *Stretlitzia reginae,* grows to a height of 1.5 m and bears bright orange flowers with dark blue bracts which look like crested birds' heads. *S. nicolai* has handsome paddle-like leaves and stunning white flowers with dark purple bracts.

Flowering shrubs for the exotic garden include the *Hibiscus rosa-sinensis,* from which many flamboyant

cultivars have been hybridised. The *Vireya* rhododendrons grow superbly in subtropical situations, their glossy evergreen foliage the perfect foil for their stunning flowers. *Vireya* 'Tropic Glow', and 'Java Light' offer gorgeous shades of old gold and burnt orange. The shrub *Brugmansia suaveolens* bears huge white or peach-pink trumpet flowers which are heavily scented and look extremely exotic.

The plant which is the *pièce de résistance* of the truly temperate subtropical garden has to be the banana – it would be difficult to find a plant with more distinctive foliage. The Abyssinian banana, *Ensete ventricosum,* is a popular cultivar and for smaller gardens the red Assam banana, *Musa manni,* is a dwarf species with rich olive-green leaves and red midribs. All banana species are gross feeders and need abundant moisture.

At its other extreme, the subtropical garden may be created from a compelling desert landscape. The

This exotic garden features a dramatic display of bromeliads; a single specimen of *Neoregelia concentra* (centre foreground) offers lustrous strap-like foliage crowned with purple. Immediately behind is *Guzmania* 'Cherry'. Tall *Bilbergia* and the silvery swords of *Aechmea fasciata* give height amongst lower-growing bromeliads. Massed *Neoregelia* 'Fireball', with opulent mahogany-like foliage, occupy the tree trunk. Dwarf heavenly bamboo *Nandina domestica* 'Pygmaea', a small shrub with narrow colourful leaves, provides softer form amongst the spiky bromeliads. The weeping conifer (left) also complements their bold foliage.

location for this garden may be arid, having little rainfall, but it will be a theatrical garden, where the players onstage are handsome sculptural specimens such as spiky *Agave attenuata,* the fascinating domed and fringed *Cycas revoluta,* or the upright waved spears of *Sansevieria trifasiate.*

Ground coverings are of crunchy sand or pebbles, with groupings of heat-baked boulders providing rounded shapes to complement the angular spiny forms of cacti species. At their feet may be grouped clumps of succulents, of which there is an immense variety. *Aloe thraskii* is a large impressive succulent bearing fleshy, drooping, spiked leaves and flower spires of bright gold.

The landscape of the arid subtropical garden is punctuated with the sword-like leaves of drought-tolerant yuccas, of which *Y. aloifolia,* with its skirt of spent leaves and height of some 3 m, is an especially spectacular specimen. A favoured species is *Yucca filamentosa,* which throws up from a large rosette of spiky leaves a tall stem covered in pendulous, cup-shaped, white blooms. The squat and solid single trunk of the dragon tree, *Dracaena draco,* erupts into a dramatic crown of sword-like spikes and is drought tolerant.

It is possible for the gardener whose plot lies on an arid sun-baked plain to turn his or her location to distinct advantage. Many designer plants much sought after by garden landscapers originate from semi-arid regions. They are plants with strong visual appeal; plants that command attention. They have the added bonus of creating a low-maintenance garden where feeding, watering and pruning are virtually non-existent.

Creating an arid subtropical-style garden is a challenging and stimulating project, offering tremendous visual excitement and scope for dramatic landscaping.

Beneath tall palms, the Japanese sago palm *Cycas revoluta* stands as guardian to a large rock and doorway. Handsome red-flushed bromeliads cluster amongst other rocks, and to the left are the spiky sword-like leaves of the dragon tree *Dracaena draco*. These plantings are suited to gardens experiencing temperate winters.

Right: *Cycas revoluta*, the Japanese sago palm, makes an imposing specimen to the right of the pool in this subtropical courtyard garden. *Aloe plicatilis* thrusts strap-like leaves upwards in the centre of the rocks, and the walls of the garden are lined with lashed bamboo poles – an exciting and unusual feature.

A subtropical-jungle-like luxuriance of plantings surround this large pool with a dreamy South Seas magnificence. Tree ferns droop huge fronds towards water afloat with water lilies, and a day lily (*Hemerocallis* hybrid) gives an abundance of glowing apricot blooms; the giant leaves of *Gunnera manicata* draw the eye to the opposite side of the pool.

Left: Beneath a sky heavy with heat, palms, the broad leaves of a banana tree, and other subtropical species, provide shelter for a colourful grouping of subtropical vireya rhododendrons. The cultivar on the right is 'Tropic Glow' and on the left 'Java Light'.

Attractively silhouetted against the sky, fine specimens of the bangalow palm *Archontophoenix cunninghamiana*, showing beaded inflorescences, tower over the spiky rosette forms of *Aloe* x *salm dyckiana* and the Japanese sago palm *Cycas revoluta*. To the left, plantings of the big bromeliad *Aechmea cordata* and golden succulents offer further exciting plant sculpture.

Top: A lush subtropical garden where palms wave graceful fronds over flamboyant red and gold *Canna* lilies. The broad bronze-black leaves of the banana 'Ensete Maurelii' (centre) and those of dramatic *Aroid* hybrids contrast superbly with the fringes of the palm.

Left: Bold subtropical plantings look their best and create a luxurious aspect when near water gardens and swimming pools – a fact well illustrated in this garden, where the bold leaves of *Canna* lilies flank one side of the pathway and palm fronds droop softly on the other.
The stairway leads down invitingly to the pool, where fiery red epidendrum orchids cascade over the water.

THE LARGE GARDEN

The grand English garden unashamedly set out to impress with lavish landscapes, opulent plantings and complexity of design. Immense sweeps of lawn were punctuated with stone terraces, urn-topped balustrades and statues amidst ornate fountains. Geometrical beds showed off massed displays of annuals or roses, huge herbaceous borders proliferated and lakes, broad sweeps of shrubbery and copses of fine specimen trees gave the garden a park-like effect.

The style and layout of the large eighteenth century garden still affect the designs and styles of larger gardens today. But in our busy world the owner is concerned with reducing maintenance to the minimum and few gardeners can afford more than a few hours paid help – the days of the head gardener and his team of under-gardeners have long gone!

Much of the beauty of the large modern garden relies on breadth and simplicity of effect. Many are created by busy farming folk in rural areas who approach design with a refreshing simplicity. They skilfully incorporate natural features in the landscape rather than imposing high-maintenance formal gardens upon it. A natural pool or lake may be enhanced with quiet plantings of willows, maples, nyssas or taxodiums, and with water-related plants around the margins. Pathways follow the natural contours of the land and are punctuated with large groups of flowering shrubs and stands of other fine specimen trees. These are carefully grouped to allow the garden to show attractive rural landscapes beyond, perhaps revealing a distant range of mountains, a small town in a hollow or the glitter of the sun on a far away river.

Nearer the house, old barns and outbuildings which are a feature of the home and garden environment may be integrated into the overall design. They are given a new lease of life, serving both an aesthetic and utilitarian purpose – perhaps used as props for deluges of roses or as canopies for climbers. Ornamental features such as gazebos, summer houses, shade houses or pergolas grace spacious corners, while a swimming pool or tennis court add to the opportunities for outdoor living. Flower beds and borders are generally situated near the house for ease of maintenance and are in a more relaxed style than

Opposite: Plants with bold flowers – cream sisyrinchiums (*Sisyrinchium striatum*) and pale yellow tiered *Phlomis* (*P. fruticosa*) – are planted in masses for dramatic effect in a large rural garden. The young trees (*Gleditsia* 'Sunburst') will give height to the borders as they grow and enhance the gold, green and cream planting scheme. Old stone walls marking the boundaries of garden and paddocks make a delightful and unusual feature.

A garden to dream in on summer days! A brick pathway beckons, inviting one to admire the roses, irises and forget-me-nots, then to linger on the smooth lawn flanked by stately conifers. Near the house, beds of golden flowers tone beautifully with a dramatic golden macrocarpa clipped into three tiers. Its formal shape contrasts well with the free-flowing form of the tree *Robinia pseudocacia* 'Frisia'.

the grand herbaceous border of the formal garden.

Mature stands of trees create woodland settings where meandering walks, bordered by under-plantings of rhododendrons, azaleas and camellias, have been created. These shrubs may be under-planted in turn with massed bulbs to delight in spring. Woodland areas in the larger garden often have a stream trickling through and clever gardeners enhance this delightful natural feature by planting its margins with moisture-loving plants such as *Primula heladoxa, Hosta* species, *Arum* lilies or water-related plants with bold foliage. Stepping from the woodland

into the garden, broad sweeps of unbroken lawn lead the eye out into the wider landscape.

When the gardener's preference is to create and maintain a large formal garden no pretence is made about the fact that it has been landscaped. The water feature may be a grand lake, across which swans glide, or an ornate classically designed pool built of stone or brick and decorated with fountains, em-bellished stonework and traditional statuary.

The structure of the large formal garden is strict-ly symmetrical, intersected by straight pathways and punctuated by long vistas. Geometrical layouts of

Rural gardeners often incorporate existing natural features of the landscape into their gardens, rather than trying to change them dramatically. Often, as is the case with this garden, a large park-like or woodland ambience results; broad sweeps of lawn planted with a variety of mature trees are divided by wide borders which rely on restricted colours and repetition of plantings to give impact. In the foreground, filmy blue *Nigella*, and silvery-white *Lychnis coronaria* 'Alba' are highlighted by the orange petals of *Eschscholzia*. The far border is massed with creamy *Sisyrinchium* (*S. striata*), and trees frame a pleasant glimpse of rural life, where grazing sheep emphasise the green tranquillity of the park-like setting.

parallel lines, circles and spirals are filled with uniform masses of bedding plants and repeated plantings of shrubs and trees which are always equal in number. These are often clipped into geometric topiary shapes or trained to grow through wires into the shape of a bird or animal.

Confined within 'walls' of formal clipped hedging, old red brick or fencing of traditional wooden pickets, wrought iron or trellised timber frames, the garden is divided into outdoor rooms which can be devoted to the growing of specific plants or to thematic colour schemes, such as the world-famous white garden at Sissinghurst or the fascinating red garden at Hidcote.

Unlike small gardens, which are on show in their entirety all year round, the large garden can be divided into compartments, in which some areas are in peak bloom and others are off-season. The latter create areas of pleasant quietude during their resting period.

Flower beds echo the elaborate knot gardens of yesteryear, bounded by low clipped hedges of box, lonicera, lavender or rosemary, and are intersected by paths of ornamental gravel or of bricks laid in var-

A succession of rose-covered archways draws the eye and feet along the formal grassed walkway of this gracious garden. Repeated plantings of tall conifers punctuate the length of the walk, and herbaceous borders planted with roses and old-fashioned perennials give the vista the timeless appeal of classical gardens of yesteryear.

Jekyll did not give tuppence whether the plants she employed were herbaceous or not, as long as they fulfilled her purpose and gave good service.

Building upon her wisdom, we plant large beds for year-round effect, beginning with bulbs in spring, roses and perennials in summer and asters, chrysanthemums and dahlias in autumn. Evergreen and variegated flowering shrubs provide borders with colour and structure during the winter. Each plant is carefully placed so that it creates a harmony of leaf shape, texture, form and colour complementary with its neighbours. Plant height is carefully considered so that an attractive tiered effect is achieved throughout.

Perhaps the greatest joy offered by the larger suburban garden is that it may incorporate a mature stand of trees, one of the most prominent features of home landscaping. They give privacy, boundless beauty of form, colour and texture, provide shelter, and reflect the turning of the seasons. The larger garden may be home to ancient giants such as oaks or gingkos, spectacular flowering specimens like jacarandas or magnolias, ethereal silver birches and lacy maples, weeping willows or soldier-straight poplars, golden elms or silvery cedars, burgundy claret ashes, horse-chestnuts or many other fine species.

Stands of trees provide a backcloth for the plant forms within the garden and give a sense of seclusion and contrast. The large garden may open to woodland beyond, so that the shape of the lawn is softened and cultivated grass disappears into its shade. A 'wild' planting of flowers such as foxgloves, bluebells and other bulbs at the point where both merge becomes a delightful feature. Even if the trees do not belong to the garden, they serve as borrowed landscape and background props, framing the views beyond the confines of the garden.

In our hectic world, the maintenance demanded by a large garden may be on the high side but the labour is well rewarded. We may toy with the fascinating patterns of formal knots, revel in the glow of brilliant and innovative bedding schemes, express our creativity in grand herbaceous borders and experiment with gardening as a fine art. An anonymous English gardener wrote in 1643, 'The large garden doe yielde manne much goode in noble exercise, an abundance of things greene and aire free from all pestilence.' If you have the time, land, inclination and the muscle for a large plot – go to it!

ious patterns. Fruit and vegetable gardens are laid out in much the same way, with an eye to aesthetics as well as productivity. Herbs and flowers are grown amongst the vegetables, and fruit trees are often espaliered along brick walls or trellises, further enhancing the decorative appeal of the garden.

Few self-respecting large gardens are without their grand herbaceous or floral borders. Gertrude Jekyll, the doyen of the floral garden, taught that a well-planned flower garden provides a shifting mosaic of colour as the seasons progress. A true herbaceous border uses only herbaceous perennials for effect and can be stunningly dull in winter! Miss

A broad walkway of smooth lawn flanked by wide herbaceous borders leads the visitor to the focal point of a small pool of simple uncluttered design. The eye moves beyond the soft plumes of its fountain to trees with golden foliage, which contrast with the darker spiky form of cordyline trees in the distance. In the border on the right, the blue spires of catmint mingle with the dramatic purple-red leaves of *Heuchera* 'Palace Purple' and the lime-green flowers of *Alchemilla mollis*.

Left: The eye moves happily along this vista of luxuriant borders, travelling on through windows of trellis, which frame the borrowed landscape of pasture and mountain beyond the garden. In keeping with the era of the homestead, the colourful floral borders are planted with old-fashioned roses and perennials. The deep pink rose in the foreground is 'Souvenir d'un Ami' and further on *Pyrethrum* 'Silver Lace' billows frothy masses of tiny white daisy-like flowers onto the lawn.

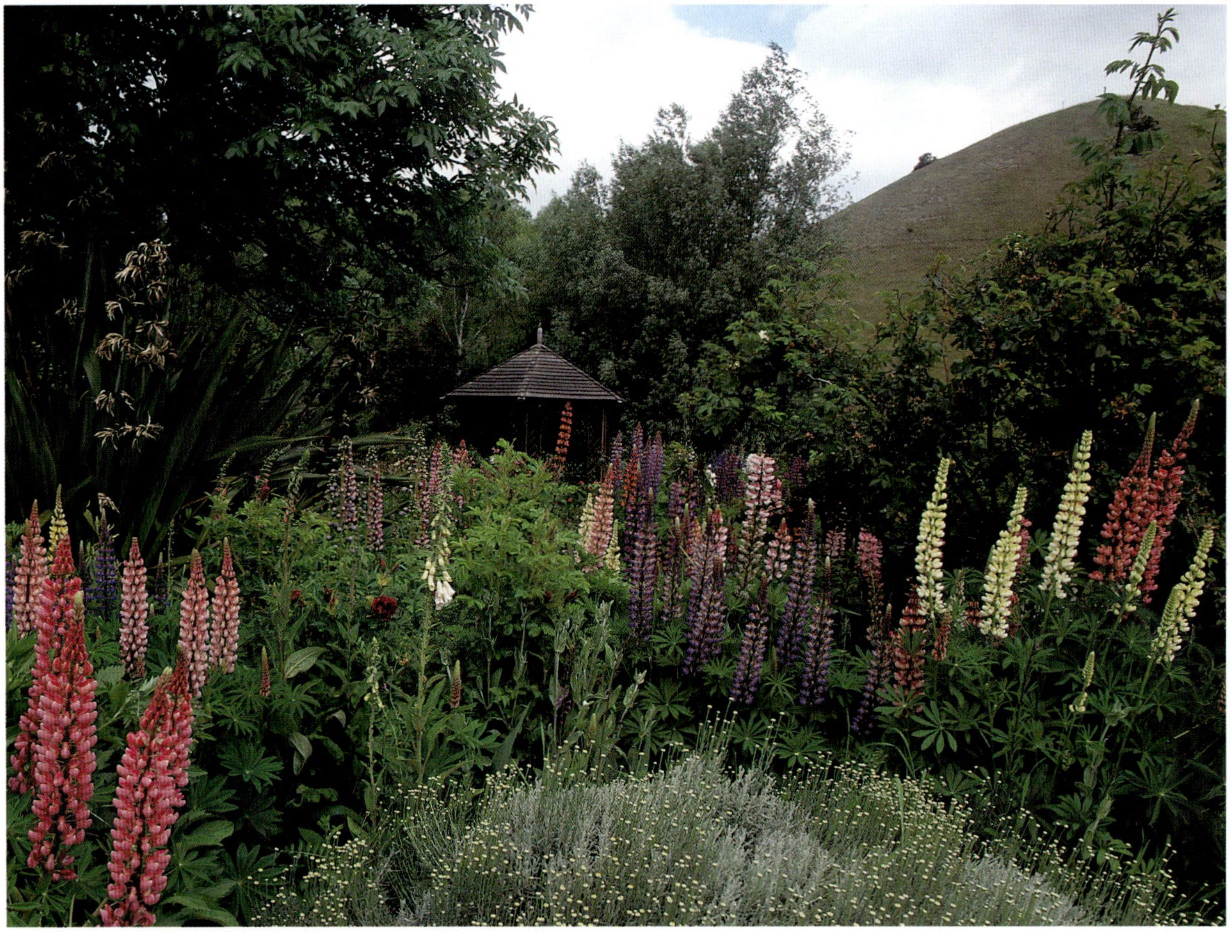

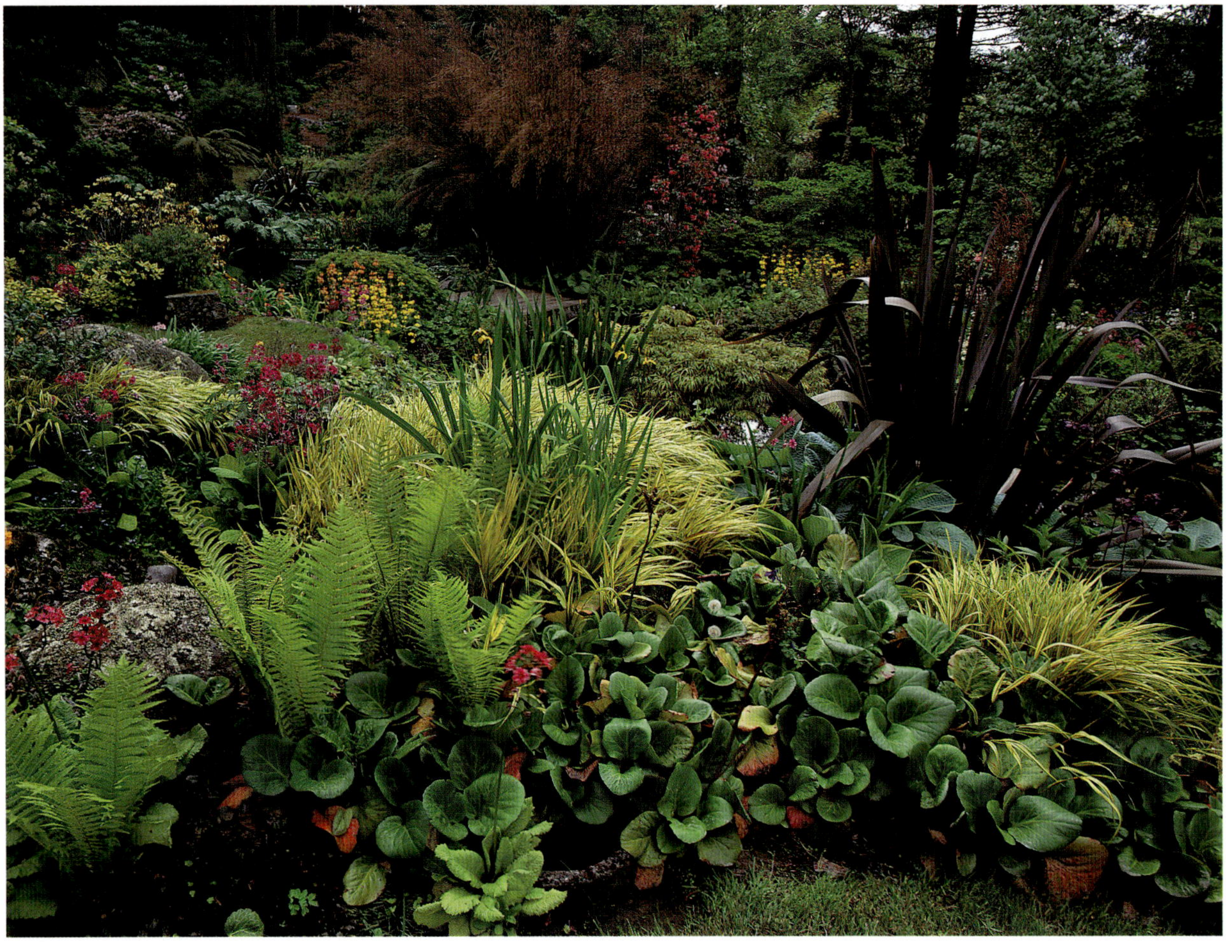

Opposite top: Silvery cotton lavender (*Santolina*) bearing tiny cream buttons and the stately spires of lupin flowers frame a distant hill, making it an integral part of this delightful rural garden.

Opposite bottom: Drama of plant form, colour and foliage are the essentials of the striking massed planting in this garden. In the foreground, the handsome leaves of bergenias complement repeated plantings of golden weeping grass *Hakonechloa macra* 'Aureola'. To the right, *Phormium* 'Dark Delight' throws up bold broad spears, its colour echoed by bronze foliage in the background. The tiered flowers of candelabra primulas lend a touch of delicacy among the stronger foliage forms. In the distance, a tantalising glimpse of a bridge is seen, where the giant leaves of *Gunnera manicata* are on guard duty!

Top right: Distant landscape has been skilfully integrated into the overall design of this gracious garden, giving the feeling of cool green wide open spaces. Planting schemes restricted to soft pinks and varying hues of green create a tranquil ambience, and one longs to follow the attractive bridge over the lily pond to explore the long vista of lawns beyond.

Centre right: Large gardens are often divided by hedges, walls or dense plantings into garden rooms or compartments. Enclosed by luxuriant foliage, this small water garden is an oasis of restful greens and golds. To the left, glossy *Bergenia* leaves and a variegated *Hosta* hybrid contrast with lime-green *Euphorbia* flower heads. Tall conifers provide stately upright form and complement the golden foliage of the trees behind. To the right, Solomon's seal (*Polygonatum multiflorum*) sends arches of handsome leaf sprays across the pool.

Bottom right: There are many inviting places in which to linger in this large country garden. The gently curving path invites one to pause and admire the flowers or pieces of classic statuary tucked into the plantings, or to travel onwards to discover what secrets lie at its end.

Stone walls divide and enclose massed floral beds from the rest of the garden, creating an almost secret room full of scent and colour. The English rose 'Graham Thomas' is the scene stealer, complementing underplantings of blue campanula and double white feverfew flowers. Dense plantings billowing onto the narrow path include dwarf mauve asters, tall lavender-pink poppies, and silvery-blue seaholly, *Eryngium*.

Right: This city garden has been divided into a series of outdoor rooms. In this area an exciting orange colour scheme is being pursued. Glowing pokers (*Kniphofia*) are aided and abetted by orange-gold daisy flowers, complemented by blue campanula and cooled by double white feverfew flowers, the felted silver foliage and white flowers of *Lychnis coronaria* 'Alba', and beautifully textured silver-blue leaves of a *Hosta*.

Below: Who could resist strolling along this inviting pathway where white roses are not only at one's feet but overhead? A border of frothy blue catmint complements both the roses and the golden foliage at path's end, where undiscovered secrets wait in the shade of the tall trees. The attractive topiary specimen of *Buxus* in a terracotta pot marks the axis of the pathway at its crossroads.

SMALL GARDENS

The appeal of a small, attractive and easily maintained garden is universal. As the population increases, space for living grows less and necessity rather than choice dictates that this is the age of the smaller garden. A large proportion of people across the globe live in modest houses in suburban areas, or in flats, apartments or high-rise tower blocks in inner-city confines. A garden, no matter how small, is a treasured asset in the life-style of urban dwellers.

Whether the small garden has been created by choice or of necessity, lack of space has not restricted imaginative gardeners from creating gardens in extraordinarily diverse styles and designs. Large gardens usually rely upon their sweeping lawns, broad vistas and grand borders for effect, so to a certain extent they are subject to the same principles of design. Small gardens may be designed with a specific thematic approach, making them imaginative and highly individual.

The small garden may have an oriental or subtropical flavour; have a relaxed cottage or floral garden ambience; be of a severely classical and formal design; it may be created in a tiny inner-city courtyard or walled garden, on a balcony or patio –

or it may even be on the roof. But like all gardens, it must be an extension of the home, a sheltered 'room' that is furnished with plants, paved or grassed areas that provide opportunity for outdoor living, entertainment and relaxation. These elements are especially vital in the planning and planting of the small garden so that the available space is used in the most efficient manner.

Unfenced or open areas designated for small gardens are often roughly geometric in shape, so the plantings are usually best confined around the outer edges, leaving as much central space as possible for lawn, paving and furnishings.

The knack of designing the framework of any garden is to perceive in high summer how it will look in winter, stripped of beguiling flowers. In the small garden everything is visible all year round, so it is extremely important to create foundation plantings with year-round appeal, rather than rely on those whose beauty is outstanding but short-lived. Plantings of small trees, flowering shrubs with evergreen and variegated foliage, or plants with striking architectural form and bold leaves will help to create a basic framework which will maintain interest all year.

Opposite: A tranquil scene in a tranquil garden! The cat dozes in front of flowers which billow out over the pathway with delicious freedom. Plantings include (foreground) yellow *Canna* lilies, grey cotton lavender (*Santolina*), velvet-red dianthus, a luxuriant clump of day lilies (*Hemerocallis*); (centre) *Artemisia* 'Powis Castle', mignonette, the blue daisy *Felicia ameloides* and dwarf hollyhocks (rear). Vertical plantings of sweet peas and a small rose in the background complete a delightful cottage garden design in a small space.

A mellow pathway of old bricks, billowing flowers, steps which beckon to a cool verandah and an open doorway say it all – 'Welcome'. An enchanting cottage garden ambience has been achieved in the front yard of this small city villa. Plantings of soft pinks, lavenders and whites include, on the left, a dwarf hydrangea, a standard rose 'The Fairy', *Viscaria* 'Blue Angel' and pink petunias. Champagne spires of mignonette and roses underplant the left verandah, and on the right are lavender-pink drifts of viscaria, blue spires of *Nepeta* 'Six Hills Giant' and the pink-tipped daisy *Erigeron karvinskianus*. An ivy hedge screens the garden from the road and provides a rich green background for the plantings.

Once this has been established, a diverse mixture of annuals, tender perennials and container specimens may be enjoyed as foreground plantings.

Trees for small gardens could include the *Malus, Prunus* or *Cornus* species, fruit trees, maples, and weeping forms such as the silver pear *Pyrus sacilifolia* 'Pendula' or the silver birch *Betula pendula* 'Youngii'. Hardy flowering shrubs with glossy evergreen foliage include Mexican orange blossom *Choisya ternata,* camellias, azaleas and rhododendrons.

For contrast, coloured foliage can be provided by shrubs such as the reddish-purple *Berberis* 'Atropurpureum' and the smoke bush *Cotinus coggyria* 'Royal Purple'; gold tones by *Choisya ternata* 'Sundance' or conifer species. *Juniper* cultivars lend silvery-blues, and foundation plantings of shrubs with variegated foliage could include privet, ivies, hollies, *Eleaganus,* coprosmas and *Euonymous.*

Attractive foliage of contrasting shape, colour and form at ground level can be obtained with plants such as hostas, *Bergenia cordifolia, Fatsia japonica,* yuccas, phormiums, succulents, ferns and ornamental grasses. In the small garden, everyday structures such as the garage or rotary clothes line may be incorporated and utilised. The former may be smothered in a delightful disguise of climbing roses and the latter boast a small circular herb or succulent garden at its base.

Many modern homes feature extensive decking or verandahs which are designed to be an integral part of a modest garden area. An abundance of evergreen shrub plantings at different levels, using strong forms, can give a fun subtropical feel which is well suited to this type of situation.

Leaf and tree shapes in varied greens and greys, and the shadows created by dense plantings, provide

The exotic blooms of containerised cymbidium orchids hold centre stage in an inner city courtyard measuring no more than 12 x 14 metres. In the left foreground, the purple-black leaves of a
Ficus pumila provide the perfect colour foil for an orchid's pink specklings. The fringe flower
Loropetalum chinensis makes a lacy canopy beneath the handsome variegated *Hemerliodendron
brunonianum*.

visual interest in all seasons and back up swiftly pass-
ing flower colour. Plantings might include bamboos,
conifers, artemisias, phormiums, cordylines and
hostas, which would provide leaf shapes and textures
ranging from feathery silver, through to shades of
green.

Almost all these plant species may be employed
to suit either the formal or informal small garden.
Clipped shrubs, balls of box, identical plantings repeated on opposite sides, containers of traditional
design and classic statuary all work as well in the
small garden as in the large.

An informal cottage or floral style is achieved by
plants with softer outlines, which are densely planted
within the framework of the garden and allowed to
billow over edges onto the pavers. Structural form is
relaxed, plant material eclectic, and the house seems
to have been sown along with the flowers!

A characteristic of many small gardens is that
because they are wholly enclosed on one side by the
house, and often on others by fences and walls, creating a sense of seclusion is not a problem. The most
intimate and tranquil garden rooms are often created
by small walled gardens. In this type of courtyard
garden, lawns are usually replaced with bricks and
pavers, and plantings of climbers clothe the walls to
create the structure of the garden, leaving the rest of
the space free for outdoor living and decorative
plantings.

If space allows, changes of level greatly enhance
the ground area of a small garden, dividing space
and creating a sense of flow; making the garden seem
larger than it is. Features such as a small flight of
steps, raised planting beds, statuary or a tiny sunken
pool can all help to achieve this variety at ground
level.

A garden in the sky giving spectacular city and ocean views. The formal lines of the design, soft pastel shades and the pale wood of the deck create a harmonious whole with the silver-blues of sea and sky. Shrubs beneath the sculpture are arranged with geometric precision and, in the background, other plant species with sword-like foliage pierce the sky.

Water is a desirable component in any garden, but it is an almost vital element in the small garden. Apart from imparting cool tranquillity, water reflects light and, in mirroring the infinite variety of the sky, can become the soul of the smaller plot. This is especially true in the case of an enclosed garden which, due to circumstances beyond the owner's control, may be slightly claustrophobic and lacking in light.

Water may be incorporated into the tiniest of gardens. The feature may take the form of a wall hung with an ornamental head which recirculates water into a basin; a shallow depression in the ground sealed with a polythene liner and edged with stones; an attractive glazed pot; or even a half-barrel will provide a home for a miniature water lily.

It is perhaps the very human desire to have the natural elements of wood, water and stone near our dwellings, particularly in urban environments, that makes many gardeners choose an oriental theme for the small garden. Because every inch of space is pre-cious, each element is chosen for the beauty of its shape and form and is placed or planted with extreme care. The resulting simplicity is what makes the oriental garden so refreshingly tranquil and pleasing to the Western eye.

Gardeners living in high-rise tower blocks must make their gardens on the roof or on a small balcony. This is where, as is the case with soil-less verandah or patio gardens, one finds container planting at its best.

Choice of container shape is important. Although the variety of attractive rounded pots is diverse, square or rectangular containers that interlock or stack for vertical plantings optimize available space. Wind hardy plants are also a good idea!

Support for climbing plants which give shade and shelter may be provided by trellis frames or arches on stout supports fixed to the roof joists. The weight of soil and containers, the degree of local wind and its effect on the structures and plantings will all need to be considered.

One of the prime design functions of any garden is to link the house to the land on which it stands. On a roof or balcony garden, where the plants are so far removed from the earth, the aim is to achieve the feeling of being in it rather than on it. Ornamental structures and bold groupings of containers holding evergreen shrubs and conifers, as well as colourful flowers, provide both a basic structure and give a sense of security and a degree of enclosure which is comfortable in a high place.

Water can be used with especially dramatic effect on a roof or balcony garden, bringing light and a reflection of the sky down into the small area, giving an illusion of space. A wide shallow container which will allow maximum surface reflection is best for this situation.

As we see in the chapters on the container garden and the ornamental potager garden, vegetables, fruit and herbs may be grown in the smallest of spaces, or even in soil-less situations. Many vegetables can be grown vertically on supports, leaving ground space free for root and other edible plants.

The small garden is very much a feature of to-day's world; a valuable and therapeutic commodity which helps us to shoulder the stresses and strains of modern living. Its importance should not be under-estimated.

A luscious canopy of grapes shelters this stylish courtyard garden which has an ocean view and a sun-drenched Mediterranean flavour. The floor patterned with blue tiles and mosaic insets makes a striking feature, further enhanced by bold foliage plants in handsome containers. Does the inviting jug on the table contain *vin de maison* perhaps?

Left: What a pleasure it must be to dine in this lush urban jungle where the plants seem to grow right out of the deck. The timbered pergola overhead and the silvery wood of the decking link the garden and house environment in delicious luxuriance.

Delectable daisies amongst mellow bricks and tumbling roses beckon from this enchanting court-yard garden. The delightful simplicity and freedom of the plantings and the no-lawn situation would make this low-maintenance garden the envy of many gardeners!

Opposite top left: Catmint makes a long-lasting and delightful border, and is here combined with pink centranthus (right) the white flowers of *Omphalodes linifolia*, yellow violas and red dianthus. In the left hand border, young bushes of box, *Buxus sempervirens*, will be clipped into interesting shapes as they grow, giving the border foundation and year-round interest. Beneath the window, rhubarb with bold foliage and tufts of parsley make surprise plantings.

Opposite top right: Even in a small garden room can be found for the sumptuous rhododendron 'Anna Rose Whitney', and an attractive seat framed by trees and shrubs makes an appealing corner. Foreground plantings include the pink-tipped daisy *Erigeron karvinskianus*, and blue daisy *Felicia amelloides* creates a pleasing colour contrast with the pink rhododendron.

Opposite bottom left: The rose 'The Fairy' tumbles in gay profusion in the centre of this tiny, almost secret garden. To the left, the old rose 'Raubritter' nods sleepy globular heads over a striking border of magenta-flowered *Heliocentron elegans*.

Opposite bottom right: An irresistible combination – a traditional wide veranda hung with ethereal racemes of white wisteria and folded into a froth of the musk rose 'Penelope'. Who would not long to sit in the shade and luxuriate in such pastel loveliness and perfume?

Above left: Design with panache and originality. This small courtyard garden displays a fascinating diversity of visually pleasing focal points. An unusual statuette leads the eye through spiny cactus forms to the fleshy fan-like leaves of *Aloe plicatilis*; to the right stands a blue glazed pot planted with star-like water lilies, proving that even the smallest of gardens can have a water feature. A beautifully printed umbrella whispers of foreign places, and at ground level mellow tiles at the base of the brick planter have been stencilled to create a pleasing feature. Plants with bold sword-like foliage, some in handsome pots, add to the exciting ambience of this small garden.

Top right: Warm terracotta tiles pave the steps and courtyard of this attractive area for outdoor living. The tiles are laid in a simple pattern which does not detract from their colour, texture and shine. With no lawns to mow and containers with plants that can be changed to give year-round interest, this garden design has to be an attractive proposition!

Above right: The key to the success of this appealing courtyard lies in the simplicity and originality of its design. Hazy plantings of massed blue *Nepeta cataria* and soft greens complement the strong focal points made by a beautiful seat and the attractive herring-bone pattern of the brick-work. The silver birch, *Betula pendula* 'Youngii', an excellent specimen tree for small gardens, weeps long elegant branches against the trellis framework enclosing the garden.

Opposite: Repeated plantings of the tall cypress 'Swane's Golden' punctuate this elegant city garden. Luxuriant clumps of silver-blue lavender at the base of the trees are an effective contrast of both foliage form and colour. Excellent design is seen in the use of tall terracotta pots to echo the upright form of the trees and in the cool grey pavers which link the grey-white of the house to the garden.

THE FORMAL GARDEN

Gardens and other landscapes fall into two main classes – the formal and geometrical and the informal, asymmetrical and 'natural'. In the formal garden there is no attempt to disguise the fact that it has been imposed upon the landscape. Such gardens are characterised by straight lines, regular curves and symmetrical balance. In the strictly formal garden whatever is put on one side of the main axis is repeated on the other. Repetition, rather than variety of planting, and emphasis on strong form are the predominant features.

A formal garden is the place for artificially shaped shrubs, trees and hedges. Other components include strictly defined parterres of plantings behind hedges of yew and box or set within walls and courtyards. There are grand herbaceous borders, sophisticated water features, classic statuary and sculpture. Knot gardens in which symmetry and pattern are paramount, bordered by clipped dwarf hedges, are also an important feature.

There is no substitute for the sweeping spaces of the great gardens of long ago, but their park-like vistas, grand borders, wide walks, lakes and gazebos are worlds away from the average suburban plot. Nevertheless, if formality of design is the choice of the owner, it may be employed with little difficulty in even the smallest modern garden. The clean, uncluttered lines of a formal design often enhance a restricted area which would look chaotic and claustrophobic crammed with the billowing profusion of informal cottage garden plantings.

Grand techniques may be recreated on a small scale. A symmetrical grouping of flowers and ground covers, punctuated by an even number of standard or topiaried shrubs in elegant containers, might occupy no more than the sides of a modern driveway, a tiny front or back garden, or an inner-city courtyard. There is no need to own a country estate if a traditional classical garden is your desire!

The design of the elaborate and enormously popular knot gardens of the seventeenth century can be easily modified to enhance our gardens today. A simple design might incorporate a rectangle or square divided into four geometrically correct quarters, with four paths radiating from a circular centrepiece. The paths might be of red brick, gravel, small pebbles or modern pavers of a mellow colour.

An elegant piece of classic statuary or a sundial would make a traditional focal point. The garden could be surrounded by a low clipped hedge of box *(Buxus sempervirens)*, lavender, or *Teucrium* (silver germander). A more elaborate effect might be obtained by combining these different varieties of hedging in geometric patterns within the outer framework, so that a mosaic or maze-like effect is created with foliage of different textures, colours and forms. The four quarters of the knot garden may otherwise be planted with symmetrical groupings of roses, herbs,

Opposite: A grand introduction to a garden of grand design; the wide avenue of pleached hornbeams has a strong architectural feel and creates a dramatic vista.

hardy and versatile. They are equally at home when trained into exotic shapes in containers or planted to form stout evergreen hedges which provide the essential structure and framework of the garden.

Pine species and *Lonicera* are also used extensively to create tall hedges to enclose walks and draw the eye through long vistas and axes. These evergreen 'walls' are also used in formal gardens to divide the area into a series of outdoor rooms with floor patterns created from lower hedges of box, lavender or rosemary. Solid walls of red brick perform the same function, and though the plantings within may be informal, their confines have been designed with the utmost linear constraint. In such gardens, shrubs and trees are planted in matching groups for balance and symmetry.

As formal garden design became more sophisticated, so did the designs for topiary shapes. A wide range of birds and animals were modelled and grown over wire frames and shrubs were clipped into spheres, pyramids, spirals, balls and cylinders.

Though such specimens and evergreen walls are by no means beyond the modern gardener, it is important to realise that these fundamentals, even with the labour-saving devices of the twentieth century, do require a considerable amount of maintenance. Eye-catching they might be, but those mighty hedges and exotic topiary shapes were clipped by hand by whole regiments of gardeners. It is best for us to achieve our basic formal framework with hedges no taller than head height and simple geometric topiary forms which can be kept in good shape with occasional light trims.

A water feature is a desirable component in any garden, regardless of style, grandeur, size or era. In the formal garden the water should be contained in tanks and pools of essentially geometric shape, and the container should always be as full as possible. A strictly defined edging of stone, slabs or bricks is best for a formal water feature.

The pool may be adorned by fountains, statuary and carved stonework of classic design. If space is really at a premium a water feature may be incorporated as an ornamental wall hanging through which a pump recirculates water. The carved stone head of a lion, a dolphin or a gargoyle set above a basin to catch the water are all popular designs for wall-mounted fountains.

The formal wider-than-usual hedges of clipped *Buxus sempervirens* and a straight narrow pathway make an interesting geometric design, enhanced by the free-flowing form of the old roses tumbling over them.

flowers or vegetables. Matching topiaried shrubs or standard roses in each of the four quarters would also enhance the traditional aspect.

Topiary, which was a horticultural art form known to the ancient Romans and Egyptians, is still a popular feature in the formal garden of today. Shrubs such as box, laurel, bay, conifers and yew were used extensively as clipped topiary forms since they are both

The symmetry and linear constraint of the formal garden (and a little humour, too) is seen at its best in the design of this maze garden, where low hedges of *Buxus sempervirens* have been clipped severely to form tiny walls and pathways. Box has also been trained into pyramids, which give height and further form in the centre of the garden. These contrast beautifully with the softer rounded ball shapes placed with precision on either side of the arbour. A weeping silver pear, *Pyrus sacilifolia* 'Pendula', with its attractive free-flowing branches, softens the essential symmetry of the knot garden.

Statuary, figurines and elegant containers of embellished stonework are also important features of the formal garden. The traditional long vistas and walkways bisecting the gardens often end with the focal point of a beautiful statue. Aged stone urns, troughs and decorated earthenware pots are used at regular intervals to punctuate walks, stairways and pools. Beautifully carved seats set in arbours draw the eye across elegant sweeps of lawn.

Perhaps the most famous feature of the larger formal garden is the grand herbaceous border. These are often double, long and rectangular in shape, and laid out within formal confines. When strict formality is required the plantings on one side are mirrored on the other. The herbaceous plants and old-fashioned perennials are massed in tiers and harmonious colours, each plant chosen to complement its neighbour in form and texture. Plantings are chosen to

A parterre of elegant designs in a formal mood requires a degree of commitment from the gardener. Hedges of *Buxus sempervirens* confine clipped hedges of silvery lavender, each complementing the foliage colour of the other. Lavender has also been standardised and clipped into perfect spheres, giving height to the immaculate symmetrical beds in which they stand. The classical severity of this formal garden of green and silver is enhanced by the juxtaposition of soft flower forms of red and gold in the borders beyond.

give blooms from early spring until late autumn. Winter-flowering shrubs, and those with evergreen and variegated foliage, become the backbone of the border during colder months of the year.

Perhaps the universal appeal of the herbaceous border, which has held its own through centuries of gardening, is best summed up by the Victorian writer Percy Lubbock. Formal the layout might be, but the effect within is one in which 'not a flower could look restrained ... a bushy luxuriance of phlox and rosemary ... a mazy confusion of everything that gleams and glows, and exhales a spicery of humming fragrance where everything blooms tumultuously'.

The challenge today lies in reproducing something of that tumultuous effect in our more modest formal gardens with a fraction of the space and labour available in Mr Lubbock's day!

A pathway bordered by a low *Buxus* hedge leads the eye through a long vista to the focal point of a handsome urn, and an archway from which the old rose 'Lamarque' spills in glorious profusion. The pathway continues to its axis, where an elegant stone seat invites one to sit and view the garden.

Above left: This gracious white garden illustrates a fundamental design principle of the formal garden; although its boundaries are strictly defined with neatly clipped hedges and shrubs of topiaried shapes, the plantings within are soft and informal. The climbing white rose 'Sparrieshoop', white peonies, lupins, the giant silver thistle, *Onopordum acanthium* and the frothy lime-green flowers of *Alchemilla mollis* contrast with the rich dark green of the box and other plantings.

Left: This enchanting garden embodies many of the principles of formal design. Whatever is placed on one side of the path is repeated on the other; and a long vista leads the eye to an interesting focal point in the distance, in this case an elegant wrought iron gate. Shrubs have been clipped into topiaried or geometric shapes, but the overall symmetry of design is softened by massed floral plantings. The warm red brick path with its herring-bone pattern is a striking feature, complementing the silver-blue and green planting scheme.

Sphinx-like creatures on guard and shrubs perfectly clipped announce the flower borders in this stunning city garden, where hot colours are planted on one side and cool pastels on the other. A long vista of magnificent lawn tapers at the end to give false perspective, drawing the eye to intriguing focal points. There is a small circular pool which has no ornamentation to mar the simplicity of its design and clipped hedges lead the pathway into the shadowy depths of an arched arbour, in which a classical stone figure stands.

Right: Carefully shaped mounds of clipped *Buxus sempervirens* and the symmetry of re-peated plantings form a delightfully balanced composition, and frame this tranquil lady in her tranquil bower with rich green foliage forms.

Top right: A bust of Beethoven rises from a delightfully dense planting of glossy leaved *Choisya ternata* to preside over the lush lawn and box hedgings in this small formal garden. The pale, contemplative visage of the musician and the creamy-white and rich dark greens of the plantings create a dramatic picture.

Centre right: A formal approach to design has been adopted in this small courtyard, resulting in a garden of stylish simplicity which has year-round interest. The distinctive pattern and texture of the brickwork – a striking feature in itself – leads the eye to the small raised pool and the doorway beyond. The box hedging with its topiary knobs is beautifully curved, giving a pleasing sense of movement. Pots are newly planted with silvery succulents and dark red petunias which will provide effective colour contrast with the dark green hedging later on.

Bottom right: Formal landscaping at its best, achieving total integration of house and garden. Although the distinctive design is almost severely classical, the sweep of warm weathered brick paving and the curve of lawns with attractive edgings give a sense of freedom and movement, and create an elegant feature in themselves. The large urn on its raised bed in direct line with the front door makes a traditional centrepiece and enhances symmetrical plantings either side of the steps. The restful greens and soft pinks of these plantings complement the colour of the paving and emphasise the elegant formality of the garden's design.

Following pages: The design of the water feature in this large formal garden is classical in its simplicity and symmetry and gives a dramatic landscaping effect. Cool, uncluttered lines, pale stone, much of the water's surface kept clear for reflections and plantings of dark greens give a feeling of spaciousness and tranquillity. The vista created by the length of the pool draws the eye to the shelter reminiscent of a Grecian temple. Its classical columns are framed on either side by box hedges, trees grown into standards and a pair of topiary specimens trained into striking corkscrew shapes. Formal design on a grand scale, but one which would adapt well to a more modest garden.

FLORAL AND COTTAGE GARDENS

It is interesting to note that the world's best-loved style of garden, the cottage or floral garden, is only a few hundred years old. The cottage garden as we enjoy and employ it today evolved in England in the Elizabethan era, when the nobility and the wealthy built manor houses on large estates. They also built villages full of cottages to house their workers, and a writer observed in 1677, 'There is scarce a cottage but has its proportionable garden, so great a delight do most men take in it.'

It was at this stage that the basic features of the cottage or floral garden were laid down. The size of the plot was always modest, which dictated dense plantings, through which little soil showed. When gaps appeared they were speedily filled in with cuttings, seedlings or plants from neighbours.

The owner of a cottage garden had little money to purchase plants, and the garden became a delightful pot-pourri of flowers, culinary and medicinal herbs, and, of course, the all-important vegetables. The latter had to sustain the labourer and his often large family, and though lavender, roses, honeysuckle and pinks scented the air, they grew between lines of beans, rows of potatoes, clumps of cabbages and other essential foodstuffs.

For the better-off worker, or for those with a slightly larger plot, the growing of soft fruit bushes and perhaps a treasured apple, pear or plum tree was something of a luxury. The lord of the manor looked out over formal topiaried parks with lakes and parterres, but the cottage gardener's view was of a profusion of flower colour and scent, roses and perennials, a few chickens and the vegetable garden. Bees and butterflies hovered and often the cottager was able to erect a few beehives.

In the seventeenth century the French garden, miniature versions of Versailles or Vaux-le-Vicomte, arrived in England, closely followed by the formal park-like estates of the early eighteenth century. But in the cottage gardens little changed, except that as flowers and shrubs were exiled from the employers' gardens to make way for grand and elaborate vistas, they found their way into labourer's plots. In effect this preserved a great deal of the floral heritage we treasure today, as many of the old roses and old-fashioned perennials, such as hollyhocks, delphiniums, mignonette and lavenders, only survived in this way.

Floral gardens became fashionable again in Queen Victoria's reign, but they were confined to formal beds and settings, until the fiery Irishman William Robinson arrived as the liberating knight of flowers. He preached informality in setting, structure and planting within gardens, regardless of size or grandeur. He drew much of his inspiration from the

Opposite: The white cane seat is an inviting proposition in this gay colour-coded garden of complementary blues and yellows. Exuberant pansies, petunias, phlox, daisies and alyssum tumble into each other. The plant in the blue and white pot is statice *Limonium perazi*, a handsome specimen with attractive silvery-blue leaves and bold flower heads of lavender-blue, which continue for many months and dry well.

These true cottage garden borders have plants billowing happily across path edges in unrestrained freedom. Plantings include the double white button flowers of feverfew *Chrysanthemum parthenium*, campanula, foxgloves, *Geranium* 'Johnson's Blue', a tall *Eryngium* and a small daisy with silvery foliage *Anthemis cupaniana*. An ivy-covered archway to the right gives the borders further height.

floral gardens of the cottagers, and wrote in *The English Flower Garden* 'Among things made by man, nothing is prettier than the English Cottage Garden.' Here Robinson found a style with a lack of rigid planning, an environment where the plant was the focal point and where they were not subject to horticultural fads and fashions. Trees, shrubs, perennials, annuals and vegetables all grew happily together.

He preached his theory of informal, natural-looking garden design and wrote extensively upon the subject. With the publication of his book in 1893, he became known as the 'Father of the Floral and Cottage Garden'. His memorial sits outside many of our living-room windows.

In 1875, the passionate Robinson met the gentle and cultured artist and needlewoman Gertrude Jekyll. In her fiftieth year she had been told she was going blind, and had accepted that she had to give up her painting and embroidery. Interested in, but not passionate about, the garden, she nevertheless made a decision which was to irrevocably change the face of gardening. She would create her pictures using flowers in a garden, rather than on a canvas or with embroidery silks.

Robinson's views, published in his magazine *The Garden,* greatly influenced her and she became a leading contributor, meeting leading horticulturalists of the day. She also met young Ned Lutyens, a 22-year-old architect just beginning his career. This seemingly odd couple formed a professional partnership which was to last for more than three decades.

Lutyens designed the gardens and Jekyll arranged the planting schemes; their success was phenomenal and soon young Ned became Sir Edward Lutyens. The ground plans of his gardens were strictly formal, leaving Gertrude a range of geometric features to be clothed. She aimed for Robinson's informality of planting and the use of homely, old-fashioned plants remembered from loved gardens of her childhood.

She took inspiration from the cottagers' gardens in her village, but she did not allow the happy and hectic tumble of colour and hotch-potch of plants permitted there. Though the plants she used were old-fashioned favourites, her planting schemes were carefully blended and colour coded. The texture, form and colour of every plant was carefully considered in association with its neighbours, and in the

A striking example of the herbaceous border planted with bold mixed colours in a more formal setting. The warm pinks, golds and purples of verbenas, achilleas, snapdragons, dahlias and roses are emphasised by the cool contrast of white roses, stock and deep blue catmints. Dark wooden rose frames create height in the border and make a feature which is both aesthetically pleasing and functional. The rich dark green of the hedge provides a perfect foil for the bright colours of the flowers.

placement of the plant within the overall garden frame. Herein lay her special magic, and the skill by which she earned the title 'The First Lady of Gardening'.

Many features we presently employ in our gardens were pioneered by Gertrude Jekyll. The single colour beds; the use of grey-leaved plants; the year-round effect beginning with bulbs in the spring, old roses and perennials in summer and ending with dahlias and Michaelmas daisies in autumn. But her most famous achievement of all was the herbaceous border.

Gertrude Jekyll taught the effects for which we strive still within the floral garden – a carefully blended picture of harmonious plant colours and complementary shapes rising in tiers from the front of the border to the back. Vita Sackville-West set the seal on Jekyll and Robinson's freedom of planting with her gardens at Sissinghurst. She allowed her plants to billow in, out and over the strictly geometrical constraints of brick walls or yew hedging in massed profusion.

These great gardeners of long ago also taught us the value of shrubs with variegated and coloured foliage in the floral garden to complement and harmonise with the colour schemes created by the flowers, reinforcing the colour effects over a long period. Shrubs with purple and bronze foliage, such as *Cotinus coggyria* or *Berberis atropurpurea,* create a sumptuous effect when used as a backdrop for flowers of brazen hues. Shrubs with golden foliage, such as *Spirea* 'Golden Flame' or *Philadelphus coronarius* 'Aureus', make the perfect foil for blue-toned flowers.

Evergreen colour within a floral garden is often provided by clipped green hedges of *Buxus sempervirens, Lonicera nitida,* silver *Teucrium* and by the foliage of shrubs such as rhododendrons and camellias. The grey foliage of plants such as *Staychs lanata, Santolina,* southernwood and *Artemisia,* mingled with the soft colours of heritage roses, lavenders, herbs and old-fashioned perennials, create tranquil and visually appealing borders in the cottage garden.

In choosing plants for the floral garden, the aim is to create an overall sense of harmony in colour, texture and form, with a degree of contrast providing emphasis. Colour harmony is achieved by plantings of like hues and gradual changes in colour, and by repetition of plant forms and textures. It need not be

Above left: It is said that a true cottage garden look has been achieved when the house appears to be part of the plantings – this is well and truly achieved by this border of roses and old-fashioned perennials. In the foreground the unusual inky-blue flowers of honeywort *Cerinthe major* tangle with the lime-green flowers and foliage of *Alchemilla mollis* and furry grey *Stachys byzantina*. Delphiniums rising through the roses give the border a nicely tiered effect.

Above right: Roses and old-fashioned perennials bring all the scent, colour and form of yesteryear to this luxuriant floral border. Flowers tumble happily into each other, creating a mosaic of gentle colour. The rose in the foreground is 'Sweet Repose', its large blooms contrasting with the small flowers of *Lychnis coronaria* 'Alba', blue pansies and the silver ears of *Stachys byzantina*. Grey foliage is excellent for unifying the different colours of mixed floral borders. The mass of striking red flowers to the left belong to the rambling rose 'Bloomfield Courage'.

confined to misty pastel scenes: plants such as crimson roses, scarlet *Lychnis chalcedonica,* dark orange *Alstroemaria,* yellow *Coreopsis* and early bronze chrysanthemums make a stunning floral arrangement when interplanted with the red flowers and purple-black foliage of *Lobelia cardinalis* 'Queen Victoria', purple basil, *Heuchera* 'Palace Purple' and other plants of dark foliage.

Nineteenth-century gardeners devised a system of planting called 'promiscuous gardening', known to us today by the less ambiguous term of 'tapestry planting'! This is the mixing of many different colours and species of flowers into a homogeneous blend. Each variety is repeated throughout the border and each plant is surrounded by others of different species, producing a delicate tapestry effect.

It is possible to avoid a 'spotty' look and achieve impact in the floral garden by group plantings, using three to seven plants of one kind. Herbaceous plants in particular, such as hollyhocks, delphiniums and foxgloves, look far more impressive planted in generous blocks.

Massed plantings of one or two floral species create a sense of breadth and profusion. Similarly, we may create dramatic impact in the flower border with repeated groupings of one plant of clear colour, which gives the effect from a short way off of a continuous breathtaking expanse.

By weaving together plants of restricted but complementary colours such as blue and yellow, red and gold, silver and white, or pink and lavender, it is possible to create innovative mosaics of colour within the flower garden. This approach is often achieved by massed plantings of annuals, such as blue or purple petunias within a border of lavender, or with massed beds of pansies and large swathes of bulbs.

Creating a beautiful floral garden is something that all gardeners aspire to. Whether our preference is for the subtle tones of restricted colour plantings, or for the rich tapestry of multi-coloured massed plantings, the great floral gardens of Jekyll, Robinson and Sackville-West have left us with a rich heritage of example, inspiration and style from which we may learn and choose.

The floral borders in this gracious formal garden are presided over by repeated dramatic columns of neatly clipped yew. The avenue of tiny pebbles provides a long vista, inviting one to walk, sniff fragrances and pause at the elegant seat near a pool overhung with the small pink rose 'The Fairy', then to carry on through the archway to discover what other delights lie beyond.

Left: Space may not allow this small garden to have grand herbaceous borders but it certainly sports luxuriant cottage garden beds. The wide variety of flowers planted include (right) pansies and petunias, mauve viscaria, creamy white nicotiana, and (left) silver *Stachys*, lavender-pink roses 'Ripples' and 'Angel Face', white *Lavatera* 'Silver Cup' and lime-green *Nicotiana* 'Langsdorfii'.

Massed floral plantings threaten to engulf one in a
kaleidoscope of exciting and exuberant colour!
This fun design would assault the senses with its
brilliance and scent when one steps out of the cool
filtered light and soft greenery of the shade house –
a juxtaposition of two extremes, each enhancing
the other. Plantings include perennial wallflower
'Bowle's Mauve', magenta 'Colourwave' petunias,
old roses, a luxuriant basket of Lobelia 'Mrs
Clibrand' and the small daisy *Erigeron
karvinskianus*.

Left: A pear tree smothered in creamy-white
blossom makes a delightful addition to the floral
garden, and also provides shelter and height.

A floral border devoted to perennials chosen for their long flowering season and glowing, brazen colours. The tall-stemmed flowers of *Rudbeckia nitida* 'Herbstonne' tower over dwarf dahlias, gaillardias, black-eyed Susan *Rudbeckia fulgida*, small-flowered red *Verbena peruviana*, red nasturtiums, hot orange zinnias and velvety marigolds. The pale green heads of *Sedum* 'Autumn Joy' make a perfect foil for the warmer colours of the other plantings.

Right: How cool and inviting this tiny garden looks, massed as it is with simple white flowers and silvery foliage. The use of restricted colours gives a tranquil ambience further enhanced by the pale stone of the diffident lady in the background. The weeping silver pear *Pyrus sacilifolia* 'Pendula' encloses the garden and other plantings include the small rose 'Swany', *Lavatera* 'Silver Cup', pansies and lobelia. The variegated foliage of a *Hosta* hybrid contrasts with the dainty heads of alyssum, and makes a bold centrepiece.

The classic herbaceous border at its best. Plantings of roses and old-fashioned perennials are repeated either side to give a satisfying sense of unity and balance. The attractive froth of lime-green flowers belong to *Alchemilla mollis* and other plantings include stachys, delphiniums, nigella and peonies. The weeping silver pear, *Pyrus sacilifolia* 'Pendula', makes an attractive focal point at the end of the long vista of lawn.

Right: Annuals are used extensively to underplant perennials in this colourful small garden. Repeated plantings of superb delphiniums create a cool colour foil for the brilliance of the other flowers. Annuals include pansies, ageratum, begonias, silvery *Cineraria maritima*, viscaria, petunias, portulaca daisies and lobelia.

THE FOLIAGE GARDEN

Flowers come and go, but foliage is on parade for most of the year, mirroring the turning of the seasons more than any other plant. For the creative gardener there is an infinitive variety of foliage form, size, colour and texture with which to create a beautiful garden that is interesting all year round. Foliage gardens also have the additional bonus of requiring less maintenance than predominantly floral gardens.

Combinations of foliage colour are many and exciting – subtle blends of silvery-greys with scarlets and crimsons, glossy evergreens with plants of variegated cream and green foliage, or leaves of warm golds and dark burgundies in dramatic juxtaposition.

For diversity of form and leaf texture we may choose between thick-fleshed succulents, the dissected foliage of maples or ferns, plants with furry silver leaves covered in silky hairs, or those sporting giant glossy foliage. We may enjoy the sword-like foliage of phormiums or architectural agaves, creating striking plant association by combining them with species of softly rounded or weeping forms. We may choose plants such as *Rugosa* roses or viburnums, which have leaves so heavily veined they have the appearance of embossed leather. Our preference may be for glossy evergreen or yellow-green variegated leaves, providing a never-ending treasure trove of fascinating foliage effects.

Trees and shrubs with evergreen or long-lasting foliage form the framework of our gardens. They give privacy and provide shelter, especially in exposed or coastal areas. They are the most predominant features in the landscape, and those we choose with care when we create a garden. Size is an important consideration, because the larger the tree, the more impact it can have, and the more important to get it in the right place!

A large garden may welcome the addition of a traditional favourite such as an oak, beech or ash. There may be room for a handsome pre-historic *Gingko biloba,* with leaves like a maidenhair fern; a *Liquidambar* whose foliage turns to fiery conflagrations in autumn; a silvery eucalypt with redolent narrow silver foliage; or the beautiful tulip tree *(Liriodendron tulipfera),* with its cream-and-green-splashed leaves.

The medium-sized garden may accommodate a claret ash, *Fraxinus oxycarpa,* a graceful shade tree with deep claret-red foliage in autumn, or a jacaranda with

Opposite: Hostas have been called the perfect perennial, their beautifully textured and variegated leaves giving colour and interest all season long. They are also treasured for their soft lavender, blue or white flowers borne on erect spires in spring and summer. Hybrids with a variety of foliage form and colour make an attractive group in this garden where plant colours are restricted to soft grey-greens and golds. The globular flower heads of agapanthus about to open will create complementary colour highlights. In the background, silver germander (*Teucrium fruticans*) has been clipped into interesting shapes, and blue grass, *Festuca glauca,* weeps attractively over the pathway.

Variegated hostas combine with a sculptured head to form an attractive garden picture. Other foliage plantings include Solomon's seal (centre), ligularia (left) and plume poppy *Macleaya* (far left).

soft, fern-like foliage and hanging racemes of sapphire flowers. The silver birches (*Betula* species) are favourites for their slender, silver-white trunks and often pendulous, glistening, light green foliage, which turns to gold in autumn. The pin oak, *Quercus palustris*, bears deeply lobed green leaves, which colour to radiant red-gold in autumn and remain on the trees well into winter. Medium-sized trees include *Robinia pseudocacia* 'Frisia' or *Gleditsia tricanthos* 'Sunburst', rejoicing in foliage of butter-gold which contrasts beautifully with darker evergreens. The silver box elder, *Acer negundo* 'Variegatum', also makes an attractive contrast amongst greens with soft maple-like leaves of silvery-white. The small fruited olive, *Olea africana*, makes an attractive specimen tree, bearing evergreen foliage of glossy silver-green with grey-white under-surfaces.

For small gardens the flowering crab apple (*Malus* species), the cherry, apricot or peach (*Prunus* species), and dogwood (*Cornus* species), offer attractive foliage which colours well in autumn. *Cornus alba* 'Elegantissima' has especially attractive cream and green leaves borne on polished red stems, and green-gold

C. *florida* 'Rainbow' has red-tinted spring foliage which dazzles with an autumn fiesta of orange-red, green-gold and wine.

Maples (*Acer* species) are small trees greatly prized for their handsome, deeply dissected, lace-like foliage which offers great diversity in shape, texture and colour. *Acer palmatum* 'Burgundy Lace' and *A. p.* 'Katsura' offer spectacular multi-colour leaf displays. *A. p.* 'Aurea' has beautiful palmate leaves of old gold, and *A. p.* 'Ukigumo' is called the 'floating clouds maple' for its leaves of palest green, marbled and flecked with rosy pinks and cream.

The weeping silver pear, *Pyrus sacilifolia* 'Pendula', is a smaller growing tree with drooping branches bearing graceful greyish-white foliage – a silver waterfall in moonlight! A planting of the cabbage tree, *Cordyline australis*, or phormiums, with their sword-like foliage, make dramatic plant and foliage associations with the pear.

For year-round interest and contrast of form and colour from deciduous tree species, conifer cultivars offer immense versatility. They are mostly needle-leaved evergreens, some narrow and columnar in form, others softly rounded or weeping and wide spreading. Colour of foliage is equally diverse, varying through many shades of green, blue, silver or gold and rich bronzes.

Favourite year-round specimens include such cultivars as *Chamaecyparis lawsoniana moerheimii*, pyramidal in form with soft gold foliage which weeps attractively at the tips; *Cupressus* 'Swane's Golden', enjoyed for its narrow columnar habit; *Cupressus sempervirens* 'Gracilis', the Italian or Mediterranean cypress, with finely textured, deep green foliage and a more graceful and elegant appearance.

Juniper cultivars come in upright and rounded forms, and are especially valuable for providing hardy and attractive ground cover foliage. *Juniperus squamata* 'Blue Star' has wide-spreading foliage of brilliant steel-blue, and the pendulous branches of *J. s. procumbens* 'Nana' cascades in a silvery-green waterfall over banks, rockeries and walls.

Among the *Thuja occidentalis* species, the conifer *T. o.* 'Rheingold' has soft, feathery foliage of rich bronze-gold, and *T. o.* 'Golden Ball' rejoices in dense, finely textured flat leaf sprays which overlap in fascinating vertical planes. Its leaves are bright green, tipped with vivid yellow which turn bronze in winter.

The hardy nature of conifers and their immense variety of size, shape and colour make them an asset to the foundation planting of almost all gardens, regardless of style or size. They have been used on this hillside to create a colourful low-maintenance garden with year-round interest.

For evergreen shrub plantings we need not be restricted to the spotty aucubas and gloomy laurels of the Victorian shrubbery! The choice of flowering evergreens with varied foliage form and colour ranges from aristocratic eucryphias, camellias, rhododendrons and azaleas, through viburnums, to hebes, berberis and shrubby herbs such as green, purple or yellow-variegated sages, rosemary, cotton lavender (*Santolina chamaecyparissus*) and lavender.

The *Artemisia* and *Helichrysum* species are excellent providers of silver foliage, and where dramatic leaf form is also required the huge, deeply dissected and felted foliage of the globe artichoke *Cynara scolymus* is unrivalled. Equally striking are the steely-blue spined leaves of the ornamental thistle species, *Onopordium*. The small shrub *Convolvulus cneorum* provides massed white flowers and leaves of the most brilliant silver which look as though they have just been dipped in aluminium paint! Nearer ground level, *Stachys lanata* has soft furry leaves, which form an attractive ground

cover loved by beneficial insects.

Golden-leaved shrubs providing a burst of warm colour include the pink-flowered *Ribes sanguineum* 'Brockelbankii' or *Weigelia* 'Looymansi Aurea'; *Philadelphus coronarius* 'Aureus' and *Choisya ternata* 'Sundance', bearing fragrant white blossoms; and *Hypericum* 'Ysella', which has yellow blooms to match its leaves.

Nature usually uses gold sparingly, gilding merely the edges, or lightly dappling the centres of many plants. We almost need another word to describe variegated evergreen foliage – perhaps evergreen-evergolds? Such foliage is immensely valuable in forming contrast in leaf colour and texture amongst all the greens, silvers and golds. Privet, ivies, hollies, coprosmas, elaeaganus and *Euonymus* species all fulfil the role of 'evergold'.

Two smaller shrubs offering spectacular variegated and coloured foliage are *Fuschia magellanica* 'Versicolour' and evergreen *Coprosma* species such as

Above left: The deeply textured leaves of creamy-yellow *Hosta fortunei* 'Albo-Picta' contrast beautifully with the delicate white flowers and deep green foliage of fragrant mock orange *Philadelphus coronarius*. Together they present a delightful composition, further enhanced by the silver bark of the stand of birches.

Above right: A group of trees with a dramatic contrast of foliage form, texture and colour. In the foreground the handsome cream and green spikes of *Cordyline* 'Albertii' complement the reflexing narrow leaf clusters of *Dracophyllum latifolium* and the rich green weeping branches of a rimu, *Dacrydium cupressinum*.

'Painter's Palette'. The former has slender, arching branches carrying narrow leaves of pale green, cream and pink, and the latter bears glossy foliage of rosy bronze-pink and green.

Trees and shrubs such as these constitute a mere whisper of the wealth of stunning foliage material at our disposal to create colourful, easy-care gardens with year-round interest and colour. Imagine a small garden planted with deeply textured, golden-leaved hostas beneath garnet-coloured maples or the purple-black smoke bush *Cotinus* 'Royal Purple'. Imagine the gold and ruby leaflets punctuated with the silver *Phormium*, *Astelia chathamica* 'Silver Spear' and whispering blue grasses, framed by maroon *Berberis thunbergii* 'Atropurpureum' – backed of course by the sunburst foliage of *Acer negundo* 'Kelly's Gold'.

Pause beside a pool and delight in the giant, heavily-textured, dark green leaves of *Gunnera manicata* teamed with the elegant green and cream swords of *Iris pseudocorus* 'Variegata', together with the brilliant, newly polished coral foliage of evergreen *Pieris* 'Forest Flame' and underplanted with the dramatic silver leaves of *Hosta sieboldiana* 'Elegans'.

Picture if you will a grouping of *Yucca filimentosa* 'Variegata' with lime-green *Hosta fortunei-aurea* as its neighbour. Nearby, the soft, feathery, steel-blue foliage of the conifer *Chamaecyparis obtusa* is backed by a stand of the graceful fairy bamboo *Gracilis bambusa*, or with a clump of the ornamental cream-and-green margined *Cortaderia sellanoa* 'Gold Band'.

The permutations of leaf shape, colour and texture are infinite – the fun lies in experimenting with them until the plant groupings within your garden are little short of horticultural genius.

The sweeping fronds of tree ferns (*Cyathea*) create a lace-like canopy for the bold foliage of hostas and ligularias. The white trumpets of an arum lily, *Zantadeschia aethiopica*, provide an attractive highlight amongst the rich greens of the foliage.

Left: A dramatic foliage garden suggesting all the luxuriance of a tropical rainforest. Cycads are the ancient aristocrats of all foliage plants, their origins traced back in evolutionary terms to early ice ages. Although they look as though they belong to hot, steamy climates, they are surprisingly hardy and will do well in areas enjoying temperate winters. They are also able to withstand a considerable degree of sun, wind and drought.

Dramatic association of plant form and foliage is the essence of this striking garden. In the foreground, the small daisy *Erigeron karvinskianus* provides a touch of floral delicacy against the bold leaves of other plantings. The attractive grass with weeping lime-green tassels (right foreground) is *Chionochloa flavicans* and silvery-blue *Agave attenuata* occupies the centre. Groups of *Cordyline* trees throw out spiky foliage; the younger tree with bronze-red foliage is *Cordyline* 'Purple Tower'.

Opposite top: A carpet of crimson and gold lies beneath these deciduous trees, as vital as evergreens to the structure and framework of the garden. In winter their bare branches let in sunlight and add beauty of form and shape, while in summer they provide shade and shelter.

Opposite bottom left: Deciduous trees are a celebration of autumn, with branches bearing foliage of gold, orange and russet. At their feet *Helichrysum* 'Limelight' offers the foil of lime-yellow leaves and *Chlorophytum comosum variegatum* – more comfortably known as the spider plant! – provides variegated grass-like leaves.

Opposite bottom right: A charming rustic bridge invites the feet to travel and explore the foliage garden beyond, which is dominated by the magnificent green-edged-cream foliage of the silver box elder, *Acer negundo argenteo-variegatum*. A young rimu tree, *Dacrydium cupressinum*, adds soft·green pendulous foliage to the tranquil scene.

Top left: This striking garden illustrates how effective plants with bold foliage look beside water. Variegated hostas, a golden berberis and dainty white dicentra thrive beneath the shelter of the birch *Betula jacquemontii*. This tree is treasured for its eye-catching silver white trunk and large dark green foliage. The orange-red flowers of *Primula heladoxa* and *P. pulverulenta* provide colour contrast with the bold leaves of the other plantings.

Centre left: The rich green spiny-tipped foliage of *Ligularia* makes a foreground planting for the bold swords of *Cordyline* 'Purple Tower'. A silver-blue *Hosta* hybrid adds further effective contrast of leaf colour and texture beneath.

Bottom left: The lime-green flowers and dainty foliage of *Alchemilla mollis* and the bold salmon-pink flowers and lobed foliage of *Rodgersia* 'Superba' make perfect partners. *Betula pendula* 'Youngii' weeps elegant branches across the unusual sculpted head on the old stone wall.

Opposite: A foliage garden on a large scale, where flowers are restricted to a minimum. Plants with dramatic foliage and water make perfect companions; the scene here is dominated by the magnificent deeply veined and textured leaves of *Gunnera manicata*. Behind the unusual sculptures on the opposite side of the pool, dense clumps of *Ligularia* offer further bold foliage. The pink flowers of water lilies add a touch of delicacy and the woodland setting creates a tranquil frame for the lush plantings.

THE ROMANCE OF THE ROSE

It is a fascinating thought that the rose is older than the human race, older than the hands which drew the first picture of it. The flower originated in Central Asia some 60 million years ago, and fossils found in Oregon and Colorado are said to be 30 million years old. Some 5000 years ago the Chinese, appreciating the beauty of the flower, began cultivating it widely. The species was christened 'Queen of the Flowers' by Sappho, a Roman poetess, in 600 B.C. She wrote, 'Oe'r all the flowers shall reign a queen, the rose – that royal flower ... she is of earth the gem, of flowers the diadem.'

Poets, writers and artists down the centuries have struggled to capture the essence of the flower on canvas and pin it down with words. It has been a political symbol and the emblem of a dynasty. Soldiers throughout history have followed, and died beneath, banners decorated with the rose. Homer tells us that the shield of Achilles was decorated with the flower, and England's medieval War of the Roses was fought by the House of Lancaster bearing the red rose, *Rosa gallica*, against the House of York, bearing the white rose, *Rosa alba*.

Today, the flower is very much present in our homes. Roses feature on fabrics and wallpaper, on place-mats, chocolate boxes and china; it scents perfumes, toiletries and pot-pourris; it becomes edible as crystalised candies, conserves and vinegars; and it is the subject of songs, poems and television series.

It seems superfluous to ask what it is about this flower which has us all enslaved. Sheer flower power is a prime reason. The rose is unrivalled for beauty and diversity of form, colour and scent, and few other flowers can match its sheer versatility. A rose can be a miniature, a patio rose, a bush, a shrub, a climber or a rambler. Many individual roses, 'Iceberg' for example, may be grown and enjoyed in all these forms. The blooms of the rose may be flat, quartered, cupped, globular or polyantha in form, or come in the classic sculptured shape of the modern hybrid tea. Flowers may be single, semi-double, double or many petalled.

The perfumes are as diverse as its many forms. There is the scent of raspberry in 'Ferdinand Pichard'; Earl Grey tea in the apricot-gold 'Lady Hillingdon'; green apple in bruise-coloured 'Veilchenblau'; sweet pea in 'Sombreuil'; cloves and honey in 'Buff Beauty'; and an intoxicating cocktail of the roses of yesteryear in burgundy 'William Lobb' and magenta 'Rose de Rescht'.

Opposite: David Austin's incomparable rose 'Abraham Darby' decorates an archway with sumptuous coppery-pink blooms. In addition to their old-world form and fragrance, the Austin English roses are treasured for their health, vigour and recurrent blooming.

The rambler 'Sally Holmes', trained as a hedge, makes a stunning
display underplanted with the taller growing catmint 'Six Hills Giant'.

With the present trend for cottage and floral style gardens, heritage roses (the old-fashioned varieties) have become enormously popular. It is not only their beauty and sense of history which makes them so, but the fact that they require far less spraying, pruning and care than modern varieties.

Heritage roses are divided into several main groups. The damasks bear quartered blooms which appear in summer and sometimes recur in autumn. Lilac-coloured 'Comtc de Chambord' and the reddish-violet 'Rose de Roi' are especially free-flowering. The alba roses are so ancient that their origins date from the fourteenth century. They are usually soft pink or white in colour and flower only once. 'Mme de St Germain' is recommended for her virtually thornless foliage and large fragrant flowers of creamy-white; 'Konigin von Danemark' is popular for beautifully quartered and scented deep pink flowers borne on a tall, elegant bush.

The Bourbon roses, named for a chance seedling introduced into France from the Ile de Bourbon in the early nineteenth century, have a wide diversity of form and colour, and are repeat blooming. 'La Reine Victoria', named for Queen Victoria, is one of the most popular, bearing exquisite cupped, scented flowers of soft pink on a slender, erect bush; 'Madame Isaac Periere' is beloved for her dramatic, richly perfumed blooms of deepest magenta.

The repeat-blooming China roses, first introduced into Europe in the mid eighteenth century,

The showiest of small roses, 'Eye-Paint', smothers itself in white-eyed vivid red blooms. A rose of exceptional vigour, it is best regarded as a shrub.

gave rose breeders the means of introducing recurrent varieties into their stock through hybridisation. Most famous of the China roses is 'Blush', sometimes called the 'monthly rose' for the regularity of its blooming.

Gallica roses, of ancient French lineage, bloom in satin-striped creams and cerise, pinks, purples, red-blacks, dark violet and rich reds. 'Charles de Mills' and 'Tuscany' both have sumptuous flowers of crimson-black, sensuous perfume and are bossed with coronets of golden stamens.

Immensely popular since Victorian times are the hybrid perpetuals and tea roses. Hybridised from the Chinas, they offer enormous variety of form, shape, colour and scent with repeat blooming. 'Duchesse de Brabante' bears sweetly-scented, small cupped flowers of soft pink; 'Dainty Bess' has exquisite single flowers of lavender pink, starred with quivering maroon stamens; and 'Sombreuil', with many-petalled, quartered blooms of creamy-white, embodies the very essence of the old rose.

Old roses come as bushes, shrubs, climbers and ramblers and have a far more vigorous growth habit than the modern hybrid teas. They turn our gardens into a wash of faded crimsons, striped pinks and sultry wine purples, and have all the texture and colour of the gold-embroidered damasks and velvets worn by Elizabethan princes and princesses.

English rose breeder David Austin established a highly sought-after range of modern roses in the

1960s. Named for Shakespearian and other literary characters, they combine all the scent, form and colour of the old-fashioned rose with the repeat-blooming qualities and high health of the modern rose.

The classic sculpted form and perfection of the modern hybrid tea rose is best suited to more formal beds and for massed plantings where strong colour and impact is required. They are also the best specimens for exhibition purposes and for floral arrangements. Some of the more delicate in form include 'Silky Mist', 'Pascali' or 'Flamingo', whilst others such as 'Auckland Metro', 'Loving Memory' and 'Gold Medal' make excellent show roses and sturdy garden specimens.

The standard rose, suited to the more formal garden, is budded onto tall rootstock up to a metre high. Floribunda roses bear prolific clusters of single to semi-double blooms to each stem, and modern hybrid climbers are recurrent over a long period.

A very popular rose in recent years has been the patio rose, hybridised from miniature and floribunda stock. Their characteristics are very desirable – low growing, compact or sometimes spreading growth, which rarely exceeds 60 cm, and they are extremely free-flowering. They may be budded onto standards, or trained to a weeping form. Their wealth of blooms and modest size make them ideal for paved and patio areas, pots, tubs and planters, edging for beds or anywhere space is limited.

Equally popular are the ground cover roses. Ideal for weed smothering, underplanting banks, slopes or low walls, they are also suitable for rockeries, containers and hanging baskets. The popular cultivar 'Flower Carpet', which comes in white or magenta pink, bears glossy dark green foliage and is exceptionally floriferous.

Miniature roses are also a favourite species for smaller gardens. There is an enormous variety of both bush forms and climbers to choose from and all are recurrent. Like the patio roses, they make excellent container subjects or look equally attractive massed in borders.

The modern shrub rose includes old favourites such as 'Queen Elizabeth' and 'Iceberg'. These roses are spreading in growth and are usually as wide as they are high, with an informal habit.

Perhaps the most practical appeal of the rose is that we can all grow them. Their fragile flowers belie their hardiness, particularly in the case of the ancient rugosas, which may be grown in coastal situations and on poor soils. Their foliage is dark moss green, heavily veined, and they bear exquisite single or semi-double scented flowers of white, pink or crimson. The blooms leave behind highly ornamental hips of glossy red which are sometimes spurred and of varying shape. Perhaps the best loved rugosa is 'Blanc Double de Coubert', called the 'Muslin Rose' for its fragile, tissue-like white petals.

But despite their many virtues, roses are not quite perfect. They do not possess every quality we should like them to have – thorns, blackspot, mildews and bare winter frames are all part of the package. But in return for the care we give them, there is not another flower that blooms with such beauty and abundance over the warmer months of the year. Our love affair with this classic flower is never-ending.

Enhancing a garden of formal design, the prolific rose 'Iceberg', trained into standards, punctuates the vista leading into the garden beyond. The purity of its white petals is complemented by the rich dark foliage of tall conifers.

Massed plantings of the ancient rose *Rosa gallica officianalis*, the apothecary's rose, and other heritage cultivars create stunning borders for the long vista leading to an arbour beyond. *Rosa gallica* has been used since medieval times for culinary, cosmetic and medicinal purposes.

Left: Old roses and classic statuary make perfect partners; the rose 'Constance Spry', treasured for its large pink flowers, old-world fragrance and form, frames the small artist on his pedestal.

Top left: A massed planting of Hybrid Tea and Floribunda roses creates a colourful border for the front of this gardener's home.

Bottom left: Renowned for its good health, vigour and recurrent blooming, dark velvet-red 'Ingrid Bergman' provides a glowing welcome for visitors to this home.

Opposite top: The massed blooms of the rambling rose 'Seagull' are so prolific that scarcely any foliage is visible!

Opposite bottom left: Old rose 'Albertine' spills richly fragrant coppery-pink flowers from a trellis, making the walk along the driveway an exceedingly pleasant one!

Opposite bottom right: The miniature weeping standard 'Nozomi' covers its pendulous branches with hundreds of tiny pink and white butterfly-like flowers. This floriferous rose is equally effective as a groundcover or in containers. In the background, the weeping standard 'Fairyland' offers pale pink blooms and the musk rose 'Buff Beauty' tumbles from the roof of the gazebo.

Miniature roses create a carnival of colour around the verandah of this home. These smaller cultivars are excellent for gardens where space is limited, and they are also available as standard or patio roses.

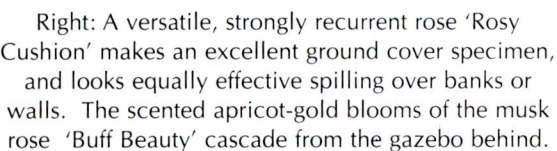

Right: A versatile, strongly recurrent rose 'Rosy Cushion' makes an excellent ground cover specimen, and looks equally effective spilling over banks or walls. The scented apricot-gold blooms of the musk rose 'Buff Beauty' cascade from the gazebo behind.

Roses of faded crimsons, satin pinks, sultry wine-purples, black velvet-reds and languishing lavender-lilacs – these beauties of ancient lineage make an enchanted garden full of the colours and scents of yesteryear.

Left: Massed planting with a rose of one variety makes for maximum visual impact; the soft apricot-pink of the floribunda rose 'Sunny Honey' complements the mellow colour of the house, and contrasts beautifully with neat dark green hedges of box.

Top left: Old-fashioned perennials and roses combine to create an enchanting cottage garden border. Long blooming *Rosa chinensis* 'Mutablis' opens lemon-flame buds to single copper-yellow flowers of butterfly-like daintiness, turning pink, then crimson, living up to its name, 'ever changing'. Clear pink 'Bantry Bay' smothers the trellis with a profusion of recurrent flowers.

Centre left: A scented canopy of the rose 'New Dawn' above one's head and a pathway strewn with its petals makes a walk to delight the senses. This rose is well loved for its recurrent blooming, sweet fragrance and pearly blush-pink flowers.

Bottom left: Climber 'Bantry Bay', a healthy and recurrent rose, rises from a bed of scented nicotiana to decorate the branches of an old tree with clear pink blooms.

Opposite: Dainty pink 'Macrantha Raubritter', with small intricately folded globular flowers, will form a ground cover or climb with restrained habit if given support. Though it blooms only once, the plant is smothered with flowers for a long period in late spring. To the right is the rose 'Tausendschön'.

RHODODENDRON AND AZALEA GARDENS

The *Rhododendron* is the only genus to rival the rose in flower power and popularity. The first written reference to the shrub is of respectable antiquity. In 401 B.C. General Xenophon, leading his soldiers on the long march across Persia to the Bosphorus, recorded that 'soldiers who ate honeycombs in the area went out of their minds, fell about and appeared as drunk or dying men!'. Xenophon mentions no plant by name, but botanists tell us that the story refers to the pontic azalea, *Rhododendron luteum*, which grows profusely in the area. Bees still make their powerfully intoxicating honey there today, and it is widely collected and sold in other parts of Turkey for medicinal purposes.

The name *Rhododendron* is derived from the Greek 'rhodon' (rose) and 'dendron' (tree) – literally 'rose tree'. Caesalpinus gave this name in his *History of Plants* (circa 1538) to the species we now call *Rhododendron ferrugineum* and *R. hirsutum*. From then until 1753, when Linnaeus established his system of botanical nomenclature and gave the name *Rhododendron* to the genus, many different names were used.

Early in the eighteenth century, *R. catawbiense* was discovered in America, and from then on intrepid plant hunters introduced exciting new varieties from Northern India, China, Japan, Tibet and Burma, and hybridising began. It is from these collections that the treasured shrubs which grace our gardens of the twentieth century come.

The genus is extensive, comprising nearly 1000 species and countless hybrids – from dwarf alpines to forest giants, such as the 25-m tall *R. giganteum*. The species are found over a large part of the earth's surface in diverse climatic conditions, some enduring Himalayan snows or winters of the Northern Hemisphere, while others, such as the vireya species, flourish in temperate and subtropical climates.

Novice gardeners are often uncertain of the difference between rhododendrons and azaleas. All azaleas are rhododendrons, but not all rhododendrons are azaleas – one of the differences being that azaleas have five stamens and rhododendrons have ten. Azaleas are generally lower in growth habit, bear smaller leaves and flowers and are often deciduous. The flowers of both species have a wide range of colours, which are often subtly flushed with other tints. The flowers come in tubular, starry, funnel, bowl and bell shapes and vary in size from 2-15 cm wide and 2-10 cm long.

Recommended azalea varieties include Ghent, Indica, Exbury, Knap Hill, Mollis and Kurume. The deciduous Mollis hybrids give considerable impact to the early spring garden, as their branches are massed with cascades of blossom before the leaves appear. Favourites include 'Princess Juliana', a creamy-pink bloom edged with deeper pink; 'Koster's Brilliant Red'; 'Lemonora', apricot-yellow, flushed red on the outside; 'Gibraltar', orange blooms;

Opposite: An all-time favourite, vivid scarlet-red *Rhododendron* 'Kaponga' makes a stunning colour contrast with the green luxuriance of lush subtropical plantings.

The massed tubular salmon-orange bells of *Rhododendron* 'Medusa' make a stunning foreground planting for *R.* 'Dora Amateis', with white flowers lightly spotted green. The scarlet-red blooms of *R.* 'Billy Budd' complement those of creamy-white *R.* 'Unique' towards the end of this enchanting spring border.

and 'Homebush', violet-pink flowers.

The Ghent hybrids bloom in late winter, their flowers are tubular in shape, often heavily fragrant and of much more subtle shades than the Mollises. The Knap Hill and Exbury hybrids are renowned for their wide colour range, scent and freedom of flowering, each stalk bearing up to 30 individual heads in one cluster. The leaves of the deciduous azaleas often turn a rich red before they fall in autumn.

Among the hardy, floriferous and colourful evergreen azaleas are the elegant Kurume and Indica varieties such as pink 'Rosebud' and salmon-pink 'Kirin', both valued for their lengthy flowering periods. Other cultivars that give excellent performances include orange-pink 'Salmonea'; pink-white 'Christmas Cheer'; 'Scarlet Prince'; 'Iro-hayama', white margined lavender; pink 'Aya Kummuri'; and 'Leopolde Astrid', with double white flowers.

Rhododendrons may be generally described as medium to large evergreen shrubs with dark green, elongated leaves, and spectacular trusses of flowers that stand proudly above the foliage in early spring. The flowers of some varieties are perfumed, and others bear markings at their throats.

Though rhododendrons may be grown across a wide variety of climatic conditions, the vireya group require temperate or subtropical climates. Vireyas are exciting for the brilliance, profusion and diversity of their flowers. They require a light sunny situation, and, like all rhododendrons, need adequate moisture with good drainage. As they make excellent container subjects, they may be grown in cooler areas and moved into frost-free situations during winter. The cultivars 'Devonshire Cream', a rich buttery-cream; 'Sneezy', white heavily flushed with pink; 'Pink Cushion'; and yellow-white 'Moonstone' form low, compact bushes and are especially well suited to container planting.

Favourite vireyas recommended for excellent garden performance include 'Tropic Glow', with its large clusters of orange-red and yellow flowers; 'Kisses', producing yellowish tubular flowers with red lobes; 'Silken Shimmer', large carnation-scented lilac blooms; 'Cherry Pie', with clear pink flowers; 'Lipstick', whose white flowers with pink frosting at the edges are held in trusses of thirteen or more; 'Cameo Spice' of creamy-apricot; and 'Rob's Favourite', with salmon-red flowers, red stems and glossy leaves.

Scented rhododendrons include the white, pink-flushed *R.* 'Fragrantissimum' and *R.* 'Princess Alice'; *R. Johnstoneanum* with yellow-white, lemon-centred flowers; and *R.* 'Delicatissima' which has stunning white lily-like reflexed petals striped with pink and patches of gold.

For small gardens, the *Yakushimanum* hybrids are excellent, including such varieties such as 'Rubicon', a gorgeous rich dark red, and creamy-yellow 'Michael's Pride'. All of the hybrids make delightful container specimens, as do the dwarf evergreen hybrids, which are also favoured for rock gardens or for underplanting taller species.

Very small dwarf varieties (under 1 metre) include dusty orange 'Brickdust'; 'Ginny Gee', white flushed pink; floriferous 'Pink Drift' with cinnamon foliage; and hardy *R. fastigiatum* with deep purple flowers.

To suggest rhododendrons suitable for the average-sized garden is an awe-inspiring task, since there are literally hundreds of excellent varieties. Every gardener has a list of favourites, but popular cultivars include apricot-pink 'Len's Cameo'; 'Fireman Jeff', with its rich red blooms and huge calyx; 'Blue Diamond' of violet-blue; 'President Roosevelt', crimson-red with a white heart; rich red 'Elizabeth'; 'Saffron Queen', with prolific blooms of warm yellow-gold; and 'Dora Armateis', which has white flowers speckled green.

Larger gardens could accommodate the unrivalled glowing red 'Kaponga', or 'Dr. Arnold Endtz', which bears large deep pink ruffled blooms. 'Blue Peter' is very hardy and has lavender-blue flowers flared crimson; 'Cotton Candy' bears pink trusses of up to 17 florets, each 10 cm across; 'Unique' offers a warm yellow, flushed with peach; and 'Cornubia' gives spectacular red blooms.

There is a rhododendron or azalea for every situation and the plants' popularity is further enhanced by the fact that they have a tough constitution, and remarkable tolerance to many garden habitats and less than perfect conditions. Their one essential requirement is an acidic soil – they will not thrive in areas in which lime or chalk predominate. They do well in any good garden soil that is well dressed with peat moss, and sufficient moisture to protect their shallow root systems, but good drainage is also important. When planting new shrubs it is important to remember their preference for shallow holes. A mulch of rotted leaves or peat will ensure good health. The same materials need to be incorporated

Rhododendron 'Anna-Rose Whitney' and azalea 'Purple Splendor' in a woodland garden setting.

into the mix for container specimens.

Rhododendrons and azaleas are reasonably wind-tolerant and their ideal position is in semi-shade with enough light for good growth but sufficient shelter to avoid moisture loss from the leaves, leaf scorch or flower fade.

Rhododendrons and azaleas look and grow best in a woodland setting, similar to their natural habitat. Many great gardens in Australasia, England and Europe feature massed plantings of the species in this type of setting. Not all gardens are blessed with this situation, but we may contrive such an area with a few well-chosen specimen trees or taller shrubs, and underplantings of rhododendrons and azaleas of varying heights.

Such is their versatility that rhododendrons make an excellent hedge or border, giving maximum impact in spring and an attractive sheltering screen of evergreen in other seasons. Within flower beds, they may be used to give height and evergreen backbone, and miniature species provide ground cover and clothe rock gardens. Add to this list of attributes the fact that the species require little in the way of pruning, spraying and general maintenance... and what more can be said?

Top left: A garden full of winter cheer – darkest plum-wine *Rhododendron* 'Cornubia' provides a pool of intense colour in the right hand border and plantings of heathers and conifers to the left create a garden with year-round interest.

Bottom left: A haze of forget-me-nots, heather, cherry-pink blossom, and the cream flowers and rich coral tips of a *Pieris* hybrid make excellent companion plants for rhododendrons and azaleas in a park-like setting.

Opposite top: Deciduous azaleas (unnamed seedlings of Ilam, Knap Hill or Exbury stock) provide a border of singing colour beneath deciduous trees bearing new green leaves.

Opposite bottom left: Deciduous azaleas provide the perfect colour foil for the soft greens of rhododendrons about to bloom, and create a frame of soft colours for the tranquil picture of river and trees.

Opposite bottom right: Ornamental cherry, plum and peach trees form a canopy of blossom over rhododendrons and azaleas, creating a picture which is a celebration of spring. The warmer gold, apricot and coral azaleas are deciduous mollis hybrids which bear their flowers before the foliage appears.

Opposite top: Eye-catching *Rhododendron* 'Sugar Pink' (right) and blush-pink *R.* 'Loderi Venus' (left) create a colourful pathway through a late winter garden.

Opposite bottom left: Subtropical vireya rhododendrons make excellent container subjects, as they can be moved into sheltered places in gardens suffering less temperate winters. The coral-pink flowers of *R.* 'Coral Flame' are set against a background of attractive plants chosen for diversity of foliage form, colour and texture. A *Pieris* hybrid bears panicles of creamy lily-of-the-valley-like flowers and a dragon tree, *Dracaena draco*, thrusts up sword-like leaves above the delicate dissected golden-orange foliage of a small maple.

Opposite bottom right: The small boy turns his coat collar up against the chill of late winter, but its gloom is banished by the huge pink-flushed flowers of *Rhododendron lindleyi* and darker pink *R. orbiculare*.

Top right: The intense wine-red flower trusses of *Rhododendron* 'Earl of Athlone' in juxtaposition with the pale purity of snow-capped mountains present a magnificent garden picture on a sunny winter's day.

Centre right: Complemented by the creamy white flowers and deeply textured foliage of a *Viburnum* hybrid, the pale lemon flowers of *Rhododendron* 'Katherine Fortesque' create an eye-catching spectacle.

Bottom right: Rhododendron 'Loderi Venus' heralds spring with a spectacular display of large pale pink flowers.

Following pages: A pair of handsome urns, deep pink *Rhododendron* 'Posy', blush-pink *R.* 'Mrs Percy McLaren' and a pearl-pink *R. callimorphum* hybrid (left) provide an inviting entrance for visitors wishing to explore this garden pathway.

VEGETABLE GARDENS – THE POTAGER

The custom of growing vegetables, fruit and herbs in both an ornamental and utilitarian manner evolved in the monastery gardens and castle court-yards of medieval England and Europe. These modest plots were succeeded by the great gardens of wealthy landowners, and design for the foodstuff garden was subject to the same degree of formality and aesthetics as the rest of the garden.

The potager – the kitchen or edible garden – was laid out in extraordinarily elaborate arrangements. The beds themselves were strictly geometric in shape and often bounded by low hedges of clipped box, lavender or rosemary. The plants and herbs were of contrasting colours, leaf shape and texture, chosen as much for their decorative value as for food. At intervals the beds were punctuated by espaliered fruit trees, or with more tender specimens, such as citrus in containers.

The arrangement was strictly symmetrical, and wicker support frames, trellises, hoops and pathways of old red brick or stone made vegetable gardens that were aesthetically pleasing as well as productive.

The few grand potagers remaining today, such as Barnsley House in England or Villandry in France, are a living reminder that growing food need not always be a strictly utilitarian business. Although our present day gardens are far removed from the grounds of French châteaux or country estates, the objective of providing the household with an abund-ance of fruit, vegetables and herbs in a setting that is as attractive to the eye as the rest of the garden is rapidly regaining popularity.

For many gardeners home-grown fruit and veg-etables bring the bonus of foodstuffs which have not been subjected to toxic sprays during growth. The tired, cling-film-asphyxiated salad stuffs bought from the supermarket bear no resemblance to the crunchy lettuce and cucumbers harvested from the garden. Home-grown vegetables re-acquaint one's taste buds with the delightful flavour of freshly harvested food, and the 'grow your own' philosophy brings consid-erable monetary savings.

A potager is a distinct advantage in the smaller modern garden because it offers the possibility of growing 'vertical veges'. Beans, peas and curcubits can all be grown on poles, arches or frames, leaving valuable ground free for foodstuffs of more terres-trial growth habits. Even marrows or squash become focal points when suspended from an arch, rather than hidden amongst leaves on the ground.

Soft fruit bushes may be trained as standards, and fruit trees espaliered along walls or frames, to fill the dual role of pleasing design and taking less space. There are presently many dwarf fruit tree varieties available which have the added advantage of being excellent container subjects. Clipped conifers or balls of box and standard patio or miniature roses look delightful combined with vegetables and herbs.

Opposite: Vegetables become a decorative feature when edged with dwarf box and surrounded by brick paths laid in pleasing patterns. Bronze-red lettuce and variegated kale make attractive part-ners; the young leaves of the kale can be harvested on the 'cut and come again' principle, making a tasty addition to salads, for eating raw in vinaigrette dressing or lightly steamed in a soya, garlic and sesame seed sauce. This decorative vegetable is also becoming popular as a bedding plant for late autumn and winter when all the flowers have gone!

Above left: Cabbages can be decorative too! The magnificent silver-purple leaves of these hand-some specimens are set off to perfection by the clipped balls and hedges of golden privet and box.

Above right: The ultimate proof that a small potager can be both decorative and productive. A delightful mixture of herbs, vegetables and old roses grow together to form a mosaic of colour and scent. Borage and nasturtiums provide garnishes and salad food, and red Lollo Rossa 'Foxy' and lime-green oak leaf lettuces are as good to look at as to eat. Beet (ruby chard) throws up stalks of tender leaves and looks attractive all season. Purple sage, *Salvia officianalis*, has silvery-plum foliage and blue flowers beloved of beneficial insects. An attractive plant in any part of the garden, here it makes the perfect companion for plum-red old roses 'Cardinal Hume', 'Chianti' and 'Marjorie Fair'.

This surge of interest in the ornamental potager is further encouraged by the delightful array of 'designer vegetables' available at present. Vegetable foliage form and colour is extremely diverse and will combine to form planting arrangements with enormous visual appeal – further enhanced if the groupings are hedged with low borders of herbs such as lavender, rosemary or *Santolina*.

We may choose from wine-red or silvery-purple cabbages; brilliant, ruby-stemmed chards; cream, green and pink variegated kales, with beautifully crinkled foliage; and frilly lettuce varieties. On a larger scale, the globe artichoke, *Cynara scolymus*, offers structural appeal with huge, deeply dissected leaves of silver, topped by luscious heads of purple-green that are a delight to eat.

Bronze fennel, *Foeniculum vulgare*, with its delicate ferny fronds, or filmy asparagus plumes make pleasing textural contrast with the artichoke. When flowers such as nasturtiums and marigolds of burnished red and gold are planted amongst the vegetables as insect-repelling companion plants, a fascinating combination of colour and texture emerges.

The day of the limp lettuce has long gone. We presently have lettuces of different leaf colours and shapes so ornamental that they are being used as border plants! Sunflowers of many heights and varieties are also being used as fun screens for the vegetable garden as well as for their seeds.

Tomatoes come in shapes, sizes and flavours to suit everyone, from the huge red 'Beefsteak' to the tiny sweet cocktail cherry varieties. There are also the acid-free varieties with skins of pale gold. Leeks and chives with pretty lavender pom-pom flowers may be planted as attractive companions for clumps of stout onions with shiny brown, sun-burnished skins.

We may grow zucchini and squash of such elegant shapes and attractive colours that they are almost too good to eat. We can feast on red, gold or green capsicums; Japanese radish; celeriac or kohlrabi; munch on Chinese cabbages; or midnight-purple aubergines. We can crunch through sweet little sugar peas, pods and all, or savour asparagus-flavoured peas.

The dull but highly nutritious beet has been given a new lease of life, appearing with stems of singing reds and golds so attractive that even children are intrigued enough to eat it. The humble spud is available in so many varieties that it needs a catalogue to itself. Broccoli and cauliflower are not only enjoying colour changes, but marrying to produce a

Above left: Vegetables are grown in raised beds for good drainage and ease of working and enriching the soil – a chore well catered for by compost bin and tumbler at the ready! Climbing beans sport both coral-red flowers and pods and, in the foreground, crimson-veined beetroot foliage makes a pleasing contrast with feathery carrot tops, onion and leek spears and red-tinted lettuce. Background plantings of curcubits and brassicas illustrate that this attractive and productive garden has a big harvest growing in a small area.

Above right: An innovative and productive edible garden in a tiny courtyard. Climbing beans scramble up a small trellis, beet, saladstuffs and a wide variety of herbs are tucked into tiered planter boxes between the benches and citrus are grown in terracotta pots. Living proof, literally, that fruit and vegetables may be grown in 'no soil' situations such as on patios and verandahs.

broccoflower – it's all happening in the potager!

With this exciting range of gourmet vegetables available to delight our palates and enhance the potager, colourful and useful companions are needed. Nasturtiums make delightful peppery garnishes, and their seeds may be pickled like capers. They also look very appealing when allowed to scramble through scarlet runner bean flowers or tomatoes. The old-fashioned pot marigold, *Calendula officianalis*, has been used for centuries for its herbal, edible and insect repellent properties. Its soft orange and gold flowers make a pleasing contrast amongst the dark greens of the vegetable foliage.

Herbs, treasured for centuries for their medicinal and practical properties, are also an essential component of the modern vegetable garden. A sunny, well-drained corner will house all the favourite herbs we use most frequently. The taller growers, borage, angelica and fennel, can soar away happily at the back, while parsley, chives and garlic comfortably occupy mid positions, and the real sun-worshippers – rosemary, the sages, thymes and oreganos – bake themselves along the front.

Favourite mint species include the attractive green-and-cream variegated apple mint; the fragrant eau-de-cologne variety; and of course the traditional 'roast lamb' mint, *Mentha viridis*, of which Pliny the Elder wrote 'The smell of Mint does stir up the minds and the taste to a greedy desire of meat!' The mint species are best planted in ornamental containers which will enhance the potager and confine their invasive root systems.

A stunning border of mixed herbs for the edible garden may be provided by combining the lime-yellow foliage of feverfew, *Chrysanthemum parthenium* 'Aureum', with the feather-like silvery foliage of cotton lavender, *Santolina*, and the intense blue flower spikes of the English lavender 'Hidcote'. Plantings of the purple-black basil 'Purple Ruffles' are also a perfect foil for the gold foliage of the feverfew – and all of these repel undesirable insects and attract those that are beneficial!

The vegetable garden of today is a fun place, offering exciting challenges in experimenting with decorative and productive plantings; a combination of art and practicality, or 'produce with pleasure'. No more regimented rows of spuds and carrots and dreary cabbage patches: essential foodstuffs all, but fold them in with the fruit and flowers!

The potager can be fun as well as decorative and productive! An exceedingly handsome, well-dressed pair of scarecrows and a border of flowers form a united front for the edible garden which lies behind.

Top left: A highly decorative potager in which repetitive concentric circles and box hedges have been used to create a more formal design. Herbs surround the attractive traditional urn and statuary forming the centrepiece of the garden, and the rose 'Cloth of Gold' forms a symmetrical cascade behind. Strawberry beds are neatly netted to deter avian visitors!

Centre left: A scarecrow stands as sentinel over the edibles in this potager. Intensive vegetable production in a tiny area such as this relies on small beds of humus-enriched soil and ground cover provided by plant foliage to retain moisture. This ornamental and highly productive vegetable garden grows chives, beet and climbing beans on the right, a luxurious looking grapevine along the back, sunflowers, dwarf beans, garlic chives and parsley on the left. The apothecary's rose, deep pink *Rosa gallica officianalis*, underplanted with catmint makes a delightful centrepiece.

Bottom left: A potager on a grander and more formal scale – vegetables could not help but look decorative grown in beds bordered by dwarf hedges of box, which are clipped into topiary shapes at the corners, and interspersed with borders of lavender. Climbing beans and peas are grown up willow saplings and sticks, and fruit trees, attractively espaliered, grow along bordering fences. This method of growing fruit is used for obtaining good crops in a small area.

Opposite: One can almost smell the sweet and spicy odours which the sunshine has released from the essential oils of the plants in this luxuriant herb garden. Plantings include angelica, fennel, scented-leaved geraniums, *Alchemilla mollis* and catmint. The tall, scented evening primrose, *Oenothera larmarckiana*, which usually plays hermit to the sun, opens brave yellow chalice flowers at the rear of the garden.

THE CHARM
OF THE WATER GARDEN

Most gardeners would agree that a water feature adds an extra dimension to the garden. The eye is immediately drawn to the variety of visual attractions offered by water. In addition to providing the means to grow fascinating aquatic plants, water features attract wildlife in many forms. Darting fish bring animation and movement; birds, butterflies, dragonflies and other insects skim the margins to drink; and toads and frogs hold noisy courtship rituals before populating the water with tadpoles.

Water offers a variety of moods and sounds. A small still pool offers reflective tranquillity, the rushing of a cascade or the tumbling of a waterfall gives a sense of movement and excitement. The peaceful trickle of water amongst rocks, the murmur of a slow-moving stream, or the swish of the gracefully arching plumes of a fountain, all create an aura of peace and well-being.

The smallest expanse of water can give reflections of the sky in its infinite variety, the tracery of overhanging trees and mirror images of flowers, people and buildings. The pattern of its surface changes constantly, especially with the turning of the seasons. It may mirror the puffy clouds and blue sky of a summer's day; take on the colour of deciduous trees in autumn; assume a dark and sombre aspect before a storm, the surface ruffling with miniature waves during high winds, and leaping in staccato jerks when pelted with rain. In colder climates, the fragile winter sunlight sparkles on its iced surface, and on the frost-gilded vegetation around the margins.

A water feature may constitute a grand lake across which swans sail in the traditional manner; an inner city high-tech aquatic showpiece of concrete, steel or floral fountains; a pool of classical design set in formal topiaried gardens; a small still pond in a relaxed cottage garden setting; or simply a miniature waterlily floating in an attractive container on a tiny patio or verandah.

The practical aspects of creating a pool involves, in its simplest form, a shallow depression lined with rubberised or polythene material, the use of a pre-fabricated shell, or the more ambitious construction and provision of ornamental fountains and cascades. Many of the most attractive water gardens occur where the gardener has been able to incorporate the existing natural features. Terraces may be cut into slopes to create a series of waterfalls; the banks of streams planted with attractive plants; or a large boggy area flooded to form a lake or series of inter-linking pools.

Mention a pool and most people think of waterlilies – but a well-planted water garden will contain different species of water plants which are both practical and beautiful. They provide colour and foliage interest, as well as ensuring that the pool itself is a healthy environment. In addition to waterlilies and other deep water plants, which have their roots

Opposite: In a garden of formal design, a water vista afloat with lilies leads the eye to a fountain framed in the symmetry of box-edged flower beds, and to a magnificent gateway beyond. Hostas with bold leaves and stands of upright irises are mirror-imaged either side of the pool. Flower plantings are minimised and colours restricted to tranquil silver-greys and greens.

Left: An attractive circle of glossy-leaved ivy surrounds this small pool and the elegant classical statue which forms its centrepiece. Water trickles gently from the pedestal on which the small boy stands, creating soothing movement as it falls back into the pool. Twin plantings of prostrate rosemary edge the pathway beyond, and floral plantings restricted to white maintain an air of cool tranquillity.

Opposite: A superbly sited summerhouse offers views across this magnificent lake in a woodland setting. Large areas of water left unplanted ensure mirror-image reflections of trees and sky, and the stark white limbs of a eucalypt tree create a dramatic contrast with the weeping branches of willows trailing their tips in the lake. A clump of golden weeping grass makes an attractive focal point on the opposite side of the lake – a place where one would very much like to be!

completely submerged but their leaves and flowers floating on the surface, there should be submerged aquatics and marginal plants growing at the edge of the pool.

Submerged aquatics include the all-important oxygenating plants which keep the water clear and healthy. *Elodia canadensis* or Canadian pondweed, which has close whorls of small leaves on branching stems, and the larger, curly-leaved *Lagarosiphon major* (often sold as *Elodia crispa*) are two splendid oxygenators. Care should be taken with this group of plants in open or flowing waterways, however, where their growth can be difficult to control.

Some oxygenators come to the surface to flower, like the water crowfoot, *Ranunculus aquaticus*, with small white starry flowers, or the water violet, *Hottonia palustris*, which produces whorls of pale mauve flowers on 10 cm-stalks.

There is a wide variety of waterlilies to choose from, including miniature cultivars such as *Nymphaea pygmaea* 'Helvola', bearing dwarf yellow flowers, and the exquisite white *N. p.* 'Alba'. Dwarf species such as these are suitable for small pools, but also do well in containers. At the other end of the scale there are the larger species, such as handsome creamy-white *N.* 'Gonnere' or *N.* 'Sunrise' with large, gold blooms. Both are suitable for larger pools since they are happy in water to a depth of 60 cm. *N.* 'Rose Arey'

is an outstanding rich rose-pink which freely produces fragrant star-like flowers. *N.* 'James Brydon' bears rich carmine-red blooms over a long period and has dark green, glossy foliage splashed with maroon. *N.* 'Indiana' has unusual apricot-red flowers which age to rich copper-red, and foliage suffused with purple.

Gardeners are often confused about the depth to which waterlilies should be sunk. The general rule is that the vigorous varieties which are suitable for large pools or lakes should be sunk to depths of 60-100 cm, medium growers to a depth of 45-60 cm and the small or miniature varieties to 20-35 cm. The lilies should be planted in open-meshed baskets, lined with hessian and filled with manure-enriched soil. Their crowns should be bedded just below the surface of the loam, and tied loosely into the hessian to prevent them floating free. Newly-planted lilies should be submerged gradually, and moved to a greater depth when new growth appears. Plunging them into deep water immediately after planting can severely check flowering during the first season.

Most shallow water aquatics are planted in pots and placed on shelves just below the surface of the pool. *Caltha palustris*, the burnished-yellow marsh marigold, is a superb plant for pool surrounds and bog gardens, as is the handsome pond pickerel *Pontaderia cordata*, which throws up tall stalks topped

with blue flowers like miniature delphiniums. *Sagittaria sagittifolia*, called arrowhead for its pointed leaves, produces white flowers with deep purple hearts, and many of the arum lilies, the *Zantedeschia* species, grow happily with roots partially submerged.

The true marginal plants are those which aid the transition between the surface of the water and the garden. They usually like wet but not totally submerged feet. A selection might include *Astilbes*, which bear feathery plumes of white, cream, pink or red flowers for many weeks. The hybrid 'White Queen' is especially attractive.

Many shade-loving plants thrive at the water's edge – the *Hosta* species are greatly valued for their wide range of foliage effects, and give variegated patterns of green, silver and gold. Few plants are more impressive at the boggy margin of a large pool than *Gunnera manicata*, which bears the largest leaves of any land plant. Beside smaller pools, the giant rhubarb *Rheum palmatum* gives equally dramatic but somewhat smaller foliage.

The *Iris* species are well-loved and indispensable plants for the water garden. *Iris kaempferi*, from Japan, comes in a wealth of colours and double forms. They require plenty of water during the growing season, but drier conditions during winter – unlike the truly aquatic *Iris laevigata* species, which will grow in the water. *Iris sibirica* is one of those adaptable plants which do well in both moist and dry soils, but nowhere do they look better than near the water's edge. The plants form neat tufted clumps with shapely flowers of blue, white or purple.

The *Ligularia* species, favoured for their deeply cut foliage and daisy-like flowers of red or burnt orange, thrive in damp ground, as do the vivid scarlet perennial lobelias which also give a splendid display. Few plants create a more beautiful feature in bog gardens than the candelabra primulas, which carry their flowers in a series of tiers up their 60-100 cm stems. These primulas include *Primula beesiana* with fragrant rosy carmine flowers; *P. bulleyana* which is buff-orange; golden-yellow *P. heladoxa*; and the striking *P. pulverulenta*, which has produced some outstanding varieties with apricot, buff, orange-red, rose-pink and salmon forms. Some species, like the dwarf *P. rosea,* can stand being submerged, and *P. florindae*, the handsome giant cowslip with umbels of fragrant, pendulous, bell-shaped flowers, also tolerates flooded ground.

While the water features we enjoy in our gardens today are certainly not as grandiose as those from earlier centuries, it is from these designs from many parts of the world that the styles we enjoy have evolved. The water garden is as popular in garden landscaping in the twentieth century as it was in the gardens of ancient Persia.

Top left: How could an urban dweller with a patio or verandah, or a gardener with a pocket-hand-kerchief garden, resist setting up a water feature such as this? A perfect pink water lily in a hand-some glazed pot sunk into a circle of *Liriope* foliage makes a simple and striking composition.

Bottom left: A delightful water feature of classic design which could be recreated on a more modest scale in smaller gardens. A wall covered in variegated ivy makes an attractive background for the pool and gives year-round interest. The handsome foliage and tall golden flower spikes of *Ligularia* combine beautifully with the delicate lime-green flowers and dainty leaves of *Alchemilla mollis*. A handsome stone frog lends a lively sense of fun to the pleasant scene.

Opposite top left: Enclosed by trees and a lavender hedge, which give an intimate appeal, the design of this small pool is well suited to gardens where space is limited. Trees and shrubs maintain year-round interest and the silvery-blue lavender makes a perfect foil for the delightful piece of traditional statuary forming the centrepiece of the pool.

Opposite top right: This delightful water garden has been superbly sited beneath tall shrubs, trellis and the gnarled trunk of an old tree, giving a delightful wood-land corner aspect. Chunky stones and fine pale gravel in juxtaposition make unusual and imaginative design media. Their pale, cool colour, the clear water and creamy white goblets of an arum lily (*Zantedeschia aethiopica*) create a scene of refreshing simplicity. The gravel has been cleverly utilised to create a 'shore', bridging the gap between paving stones and pool. The lush green woodland effects are maintained year round by the planting of evergreens.

Opposite bottom left: An amusing and highly original terracotta sculpture creates the focal point of this beautifully landscaped small water garden. Recycled water flutes from curving shelves to spill back into the pool, and the ever-decreasing circles of brickwork, box hedging and the base of the pool impart a delightful sense of movement. With the exception of a few pink highlights, the colours of plantings have been restricted to whites and dark greens to maintain an air of cool tranquillity.

Opposite bottom right: The tiered effect of a tall city home is cleverly reflected in the design of this innovative water feature. Originating from a source under the deck, and channelled through bevelled stone, the effect of a wall of water has been created. On the left of the pool, the large glossy leaves of *Bergenia* illustrate how well bold foliage and water associate. In the background, *Astilbe* 'White Queen' throws up truly royal plumes.

The classical design of this beautifully landscaped pool has universal appeal. Aged stone obelisks punctuate the sides and restricted plantings maximise reflections of house and sky on the water's surface. The length of the pool creates a long vista, drawing the eye through a corridor of topiaried shrubs to rest on the focal point of an elegant statue set in an alcove. Well-groomed hedges clipped into geometric shapes complement the formal lines of the pool, and the butter-yellow foliage of *Robinia pseudocacia* 'Frisia' highlights the rich dark greens of lawns and hedges.

Right: Animals make a delightful addition to an ornamental pool of classical design in a cottage garden setting. Fantail pigeons hover over a birdbath and the plumes of a fountain arch gently back into the pool. The mellow warmth of the bricks, the traditional statuary and the still water mirroring the sky combine with the informal freedom of the flower plantings to present a delightful scene.

Simple uncluttered lines and large areas of water left free for reflections of the sky gives this water feature a feeling of freedom, wide open spaces and year-round appeal. The use of mellow red brick gives a welcoming effect, and plantings restricted to soft woodland greens provide a feeling of restfulness.

Left: A lush subtropical feeling is given by the luxuriant plantings around this larger water garden. The attractive aquatic plant in the foreground is pond pickerel, *Pontederia cordata*. Rising above the water, lotus flowers *Nelumbo nuciferum* and their giant leaf pads provide an exotic feature. Other plantings include shade-giving tree ferns, spiky silver-green *Agave attenuata*, colourful variegated phormiums and lower growing conifers of gold and silver tones. The red lacquered seat creates an interesting focal point and provides a complementary colour contrast with the abundance of rich green foliage.

Top left: This tranquil water garden illustrates the effectiveness of incorporating natural features already present in the landscape into the design. The gardener has enhanced the aspect of the small stream flowing through a woodland glade by planting moisture-loving plants in pockets along its banks. The garden is otherwise left very much as nature intended. Apart from a warming highlight of gold provided by the flowers of *Primula heladoxa*, the natural greens of the woodland location predominate.

Below: One can almost feel the delicious cool of the spray rising from this small waterfall as it tumbles through its rocky channel. On the left, luxuriant plantings of tree ferns *Cyathea* harmonise beautifully with the rocks and water. On the right, other plants which associate well with water include a maple with finely dissected foliage, ferns, hostas and astilbes. In the foreground, the bog buttercup, *Caltha palustris*, provides large glossy foliage.

Bottom left: The main feature of this stunning water garden is the wall of colour provided by *Clematis montana rubens* and 'Tetrarose', together with a spectacular series of waterfalls which cascade from the top of a steep bank into interlinking pools below. The design illustrates how a visionary gardener has utilised natural features already present; in this case a sloping gradient into which water terraces have been cut. Plantings of pink and white *Iris* species and other flowers of soft colours complement the clematis.

Opposite: A tranquil, flowing waterway set in a garden of luxuriant plantings and cool green woodland. The bold leaves of *Hosta* hybrids, tiered pink flowers of candelabra primula and stately moisture-loving irises make the perfect frame for a very inviting picture.

Lush moisture-loving plantings ensure that this large rural water garden offers year-round interest. The birch trees, *Betula* 'Jacquemontii', offer beauty of bark, twigs and branches during winter. Hostas with bold foliage include the large silver-leaved *Hosta sieboldiana* 'Elegans' and cream-edged-green 'Frances Williams'. *Ligularia* 'The Rocket' throws up striking black flower spikes and orange-gold *Primula heladoxa*, golden berberis, astilbes, foxgloves and iris varieties ensure interest throughout the seasons. The pale arum lily, *Zantedeschia aethiopica*, provides cool colour, and the giant leaves of *Gunnera manicata* form a dramatic mound on the opposite bank.

Right: The design of this larger water garden is imaginative and eclectic in concept. The pavilion of Chinese lacquer red shaded by the graceful weeping golden stemmed willow, *Salix vitellina pendula*, gives an oriental aspect. An ambience further enhanced by exotic cream lotus flowers and their silvery, plate-like leaves, which rise above the water. Variegated phormiums and the bronze-red spiky foliage of *Cordyline* 'Purple Tower' make an architectural statement against the weeping gold foliage of conifers and ornamental grasses. The use of dark red scoria as a walking media on pathways round the pool creates an attractive feature.

GARDENING WITH CONTAINERS

The immense versatility offered by gardening in containers ensures that it gains ever-increasing popularity in the garden scene. As space for homes and gardens becomes more and more at a premium, houses become smaller and a great proportion of the world's population live in flats in high-rise buildings and in small urban dwellings. The only space available for a garden may be at best a tiny 'pocket handkerchief' of soil, or a small balcony, terrace or patio. In such locations, plantings in window boxes, hanging baskets and containers offer the means for the therapeutic experience of gardening where no soil exists. Such plantings bring colour and beauty to the face of bleak office blocks and crowded inner-city dwellings. In larger or rural gardens, containers become an attractive feature, enhancing the style and structure of the whole.

Container gardening is enjoyed world-wide, but perhaps never more so than in locations where harsh climatic conditions prevail. In hot arid areas succulents, including the cacti species, make perfect container specimens. Their modest feeding and watering requirements make little demand upon the gardener. In countries where harsh winters predominate, the containers may be planted with cold-hardy species, or moved into shelter during the most extreme weather.

Container gardening has been as widely practised and valued in centuries past as it is in our modern world. Ancient Chinese and Asian peoples grew shrubs and other plants in pots, and evolved the art of training small trees to become bonsai specimens. A queen of Egypt who reigned around 1500 B.C. grew plants in pots and sent out explorers to find new specimens. A carved screen depicting containerised shrubs and flowers adorns her tomb. The Hanging Gardens of Babylon, one of the wonders of the ancient world, depended largely for effect on plants in porous pots. King Solomon of Israel, a keen gardener, had many rooms in his palace decorated with rare and special species.

The word 'greenhouse' is said to have come from seventeenth-century Europe, where it was the fashion to grow 'tender greens', such as citrus fruits, in handsome containers of lead, marble, stone and terracotta. These would be removed to 'greenhouses' during winter – the Palace of Versailles boasted hundreds of orange trees growing in silver pots as a feature of the summer garden. The Victorian and Edwardian eras brought in conservatories, garden rooms and orangeries crammed with exotic and tender plants, and the fashion for covering window sills, mantelpieces and furniture surfaces with potted plants of all varieties.

We have a similarly wide and (fortunately) less expensive range of containers at our disposal today, composed of plastic, wood, terracotta, concrete, wire and basketware. Whatever the material, they need to be able to withstand frequent waterings, be strong enough not to disintegrate during moving and be complementary to the plants they display and the situations they furnish.

Opposite: Hostas, fuschias, perlargoniums, phormiums and a yellow marguerite daisy combine to create a well-balanced composition and welcoming doorways for visitors.

Hanging baskets become an art form! A floral extravaganza of airborne fuschias, lobelias, geraniums and begonias cascade into climbing roses against an old stone wall. Wine half-barrels also make attractive containers, and they, like the tiny road-front border, are awash with petunias and lobelia.

Window boxes are the most popular form of container gardening for adorning the facades of buildings. The boxes are usually made of plastic or wood, though the latter becomes heavy when fully planted and wet. Most troughs for window boxes are designed with a planting depth of 40–50 cm to accommodate root growth. Ideally they should be constructed with double walls, leaving a space of some 3 cm between. The gap is packed with damp sphagnum moss or peat to insulate the potting mix and roots of plants in the inner box. This type of construction helps maintain moisture in hot climates and prevents roots freezing in colder climates.

Hanging baskets are also extremely popular for exterior decoration – they are almost an art form in Europe! Planter baskets are usually made of plastic or light wire, but may also be made of wood. Success with hanging baskets, as with all container plantings, is especially dependent on the use of a suitable combination of liners, moisturising agents and the correct potting mix. Basket liners may be made of pre-cut coconut matting, compressed woollen felt, absorbent capillary matting or the more traditional sphagnum moss. A new product called 'Terraseal' is available for reducing moisture loss from all forms of containers. The clay-based material should be painted onto the inside lining of the pots, boxes and baskets, leaving a small hole at the base to allow excess water to drain away.

Most horticultural suppliers offer ready-mixed potting mediums. These contain water storage granules, a feature which has revolutionised the art of container gardening, as it minimises the time and labour formerly spent in watering. The granules are marketed under the name 'Crystal Rain' or 'Liquid Rain'. They must be mixed with water, which causes them to swell to several times their original size. Once fully expanded (which takes about two hours), they may be incorporated into the potting mix. The idea is that the plant roots will penetrate the jelly-like

Above left: Plants with bold, spiky foliage and dramatic form give this sun-drenched courtyard an exciting subtropical feel. The sword-like leaves of the dragon tree, *Dracaena draco*, stand alert over cacti and palms and *Bougainvillaea* 'Scarlett O'Hara' flaunts flamboyant flowers in the background. Containers and tiles painted to match add further panache to this original container garden.

Above right: The stylish simplicity of this attractive courtyard is enhanced by shrubs in containers trained into standards underplanted with catmint *Nepeta cataria*. A strong visual link is created between the warm colour of the containers and the bricks, and between the repeated plantings of catmint in the pots and in the borders.

granules and extract moisture as they require it.

Although most commercially-prepared potting mixes contain enough slow-release fertiliser granules to sustain plants for 3-4 months, regular application of a liquid feeding agent such as Phostrogen, Nitrosol or Thrive ensures well-fed plants which will last a lot longer. Deadheading blooms and checking for pests will also keep the containers looking floriferous and healthy.

It is wise to give thought to the safety aspect of gardens in window boxes and hanging baskets. They become heavy when wet, and care must be taken that the screws, brackets and hooks supporting them are firmly secured. Wind is also a hazard, and has been known to hurl hanging baskets through windows, so fairly sheltered sites are best.

The choice of plants for containers is extraordinarily diverse, ranging from a mature tree to a tiny alpine – almost anything is possible! But time-honoured favourites, especially for window boxes

and hanging baskets, include geraniums, daisies, petunias, lobelia and alyssum, violas, impatiens, verbenas, fuschias and many other free-flowering species.

Year-round interest may be maintained with foliage plants such as variegated ivies and periwinkles. *Helichrysum petiolare* has trailing stems of soft grey and *H. p.* 'Limelight' has leaves of pale lemon; both look attractive in all seasons. Almost any style of container may be planted with a wide variety of bulbs, heathers and dwarf conifers of softer, spreading form to provide colour on the darkest winter day.

There is a vast choice of styles and materials available in pots and tubs for free-standing containers. These range from ordinary plastic planters to handsome and expensive glazed jars, decorated terracotta pots and hand-painted vases. Free-standing containers offer immense versatility in that they may be moved to provide focal points of colour and foliage in all locations and seasons. Pots containing

A wisteria-framed doorway, and harmoniously colour linked container plantings and furnishings create a stylish and inviting entrance to this home. Creamy-lemon spires of mignonette growing up from blue-grey paving tiles make a delightful foreground planting for glazed white pots planted with vibrant blue petunias and *Lavandula dentata* trained into elegant standards.

Opposite top: An elegant urn of classical design planted with the silvery *Astelia chathamica* 'Silver Spear' creates a strong focal point in this intimate courtyard garden. Plantings which have been restricted to a restful combination of cool blues and greens include catmint, agapanthus, iris, scabiosa and the geranium 'Johnson's Blue'.

Opposite bottom: Plants in containers are used to enhance and punctuate this long vista through herbaceous borders in a garden of formal design.

plants which have passed their peak flowering period may be removed and replaced with newly planted ones.

The availability of large pots, crates, barrels and tubs in a variety of materials enables the container gardener to incorporate large trees and flowering shrubs into the gardening scheme. Large containers holding mature specimens may be difficult to move; a simple trolley made of a flat piece of wood fitted with four furniture castors and a rope handle can be a great help in preventing back injury. Tilt one side of the container up, push the trolley under, then ease the other side of the pot on.

In addition to the traditional window box, pot and hanging basket containers, innovative plantings can be made in such diverse receptacles as old kettles, teapots, boots, wheelbarrows, bird cages, tree roots, churns, sinks, and even old baths and boats! Golden and burnt-orange nasturtiums planted in old copper kitchenware are a popular container combination in England and Europe.

The immense versatility offered by container gardening is perhaps best illustrated by the ease with which a fruit, vegetable and herb garden can be grown in a soil-less location. There is a delightful range of grafted dwarf fruit trees now available that have been bred for growing in containers, so even inner-city tower block gardeners can own their own fruit tree, delight in its blossom and pick their own fruit!

Tomatoes, squash, cucumbers and zucchini can be grown in commercially prepared 'Growbags'. Lettuce, radishes, spring onions, herbs and other salad stuffs may be raised in window boxes; potatoes in old crates or tubs; and strawberries in barrels, strawberry planters or hanging baskets.

A container garden is possible in any location and climatic extreme and the choice of style for receptacle and planting materials is infinite.

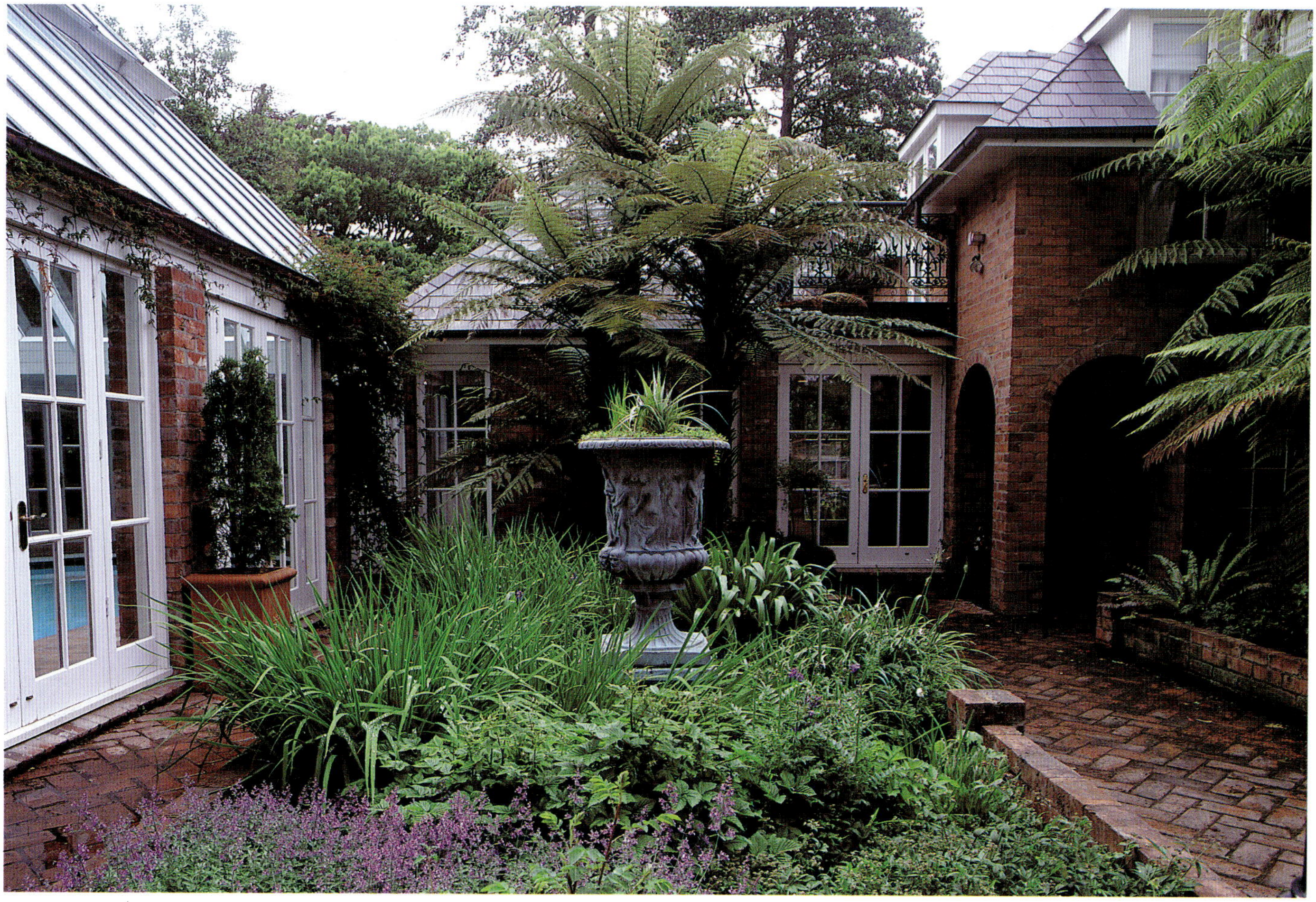

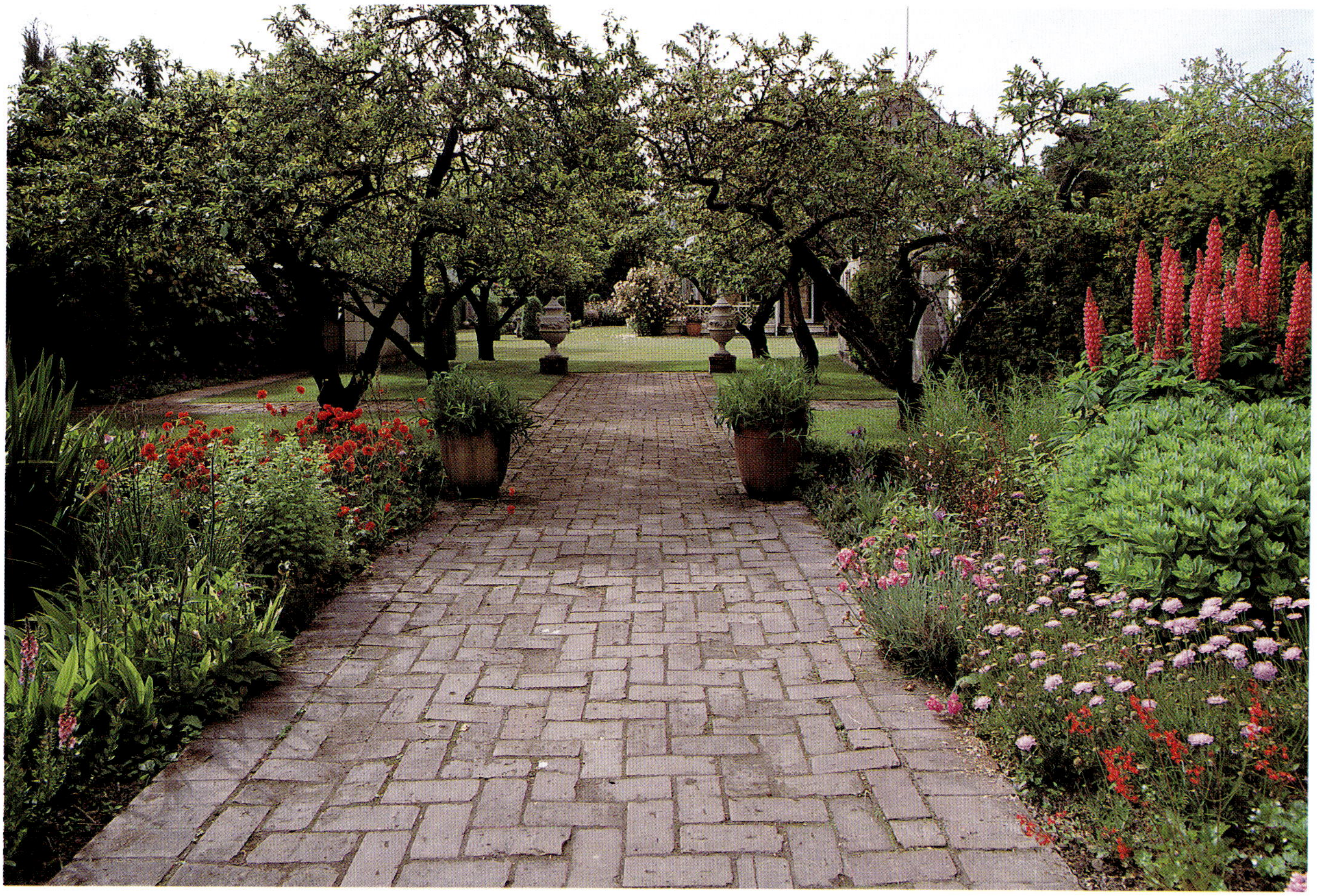

Top left: A window box crammed with trailing lobelia and a white marguerite daisy – flowers with refreshing simplicity – creates a pleasing picture on a house front.

Top right: Looking like a scene from the canvas of an old Dutch master, a potted spider plant *Chlorophytum comosum variegatum* cascades over the back of an antique chair of intriguing design. A pair of old clogs forms a delightful visual link with the chair, creating a highly original and unusual composition. The bold upright leaves of bromeliads contrast with the softer forms of the other plantings.

Above left: Maximum visual impact is created by this design of striking simplicity. A rengarenga lily, *Arthropodium cirratum*, in a container stands in a handsome cluster of others around its base. The plants' rich dark green strap-like foliage and abundance of delicate white flowers, together with the container, create a simple and enchanting composition.

Above right: A hanging basket planted with begonia cultivars creates an attractive and colourful picture. These flowers give their all in a semi-shaded position.

Opposite: The exotic flowers of a cymbidium orchid in juxtaposition with the more delicate blooms of pansies and dwarf hebes create a fun container garden with a predominantly blue and yellow colour theme.

ORNAMENTAL STRUCTURES

Secrecy and surprise within a garden are two of the most desirable aspects in the overall design. A garden that reveals all at a glance, no matter how spectacular it may be, leaves the beholder wondering if it is worth the effort of walking around it. The garden that only slowly yields its secrets, revealing secluded corners, meandering pathways and attractive garden structures, excites curiosity and maintains interest.

Combined with the more practical function of providing shade and shelter, arbours, pergolas, gazebos and summer houses also bring a feeling of intimacy and secrecy into the garden. They are structures which provide opportunity for the fullest enjoyment of outdoor living. The garden must be more than an area of lawns, flower beds, paving and fencing. It must provide secluded places and quiet retreats where people can sit, eat a meal, read a book, enjoy conversation or sunbathe in shelter and privacy.

Pergolas and archways have been an important element in garden design since ancient times. From their early beginnings as simple shelters from the elements, they have developed into structures that are both ornamental and utilitarian. Murals at Pompeii show that the Romans built pergolas on a grandiose scale – in extreme cases long and wide enough for horses to be given a daily gallop in their shade!

Pergolas are used extensively in warm Mediterranean climates and in other hot areas of the world. Often clothed with dense coverings of vines and other climbers, they form deliciously cool corridors which provide relief from scorching air and harsh sunlight. They also perform the important function of creating visual links between separate buildings, such as house and garage, and increase the apparent size of a small garden. It is a principle of design that overhead enclosures make floorscapes seem larger.

Throughout gardening history there have been many designs for pergolas and archways, but their basic structure comprises a timber canopy of straight wooden struts balanced on poles or pillars of timber, plaster, brick or, in the case of more modern designs, metal tubes. The sides may be enclosed with trellis, which provides support for the plantings, and allows penetration of light and air while excluding the burning rays of the sun.

As pergolas and archways are an important visual point, they must be placed and planted with care. Draped with beautiful plants, they add a design dimension of their own to the garden, enclosing one in a perfumed atmosphere of flower and foliage. The fragrant air and subdued light within a well-clad pergola has the effect of making the rest of the garden seem bigger and brighter when one steps from beneath its leafy shade.

Opposite: The elements of wood, water and stone are perfectly combined in the design and setting of this gazebo with rustic appeal. The roof is attractively shingled with wooden tiles and seats within provide views of stunning reflections on the water's surface, left unplanted for maximum effect.

Trellis lathes of natural wood have been utilised against a plain white background to create a striking design feature. The arched roof sections give height and frame the focal point of a handsome statue in an alcove. Glass floor tiles make an unusual ornamental feature, linking with the geometric shapes of the trellis. The overall colour scheme of old gold, yellow, white and greens is restful and in harmony with the greenish cast of the floor surface.

The range of climbing plants that can be used for cover is so diverse that one is almost spoilt for choice. Vines are a traditional favourite, as their thick foliage provides dense shade during hotter months, and their deciduous nature means they allow in the light and warmth of the sun during winter. Climbing roses, too, are immensely popular due to their beauty of form and their fragrance. Those with dark glossy foliage and delicious perfume include the coppery pink 'Albertine' and the lusty 'Paul's Himalayan musk'; the repeat-flowering, clear pink 'Bantry Bay'; and the creamy white 'Madam Alfred Carriere'.

Pergola archways provide the perfect setting for stunning combinations of roses and *Clematis*. The inky-purple flowers of *Clematis* 'Etoile Violette' grown through the coppery blooms of 'Souvenir de Madame Leonie Viennot' makes a perfect partnership. The handsome *Clematis* 'Henryii', creamy-white and bossed with burnished brown stamens, forms an irresistible combination with the apricot-gold blooms of the rose 'Buff Beauty'. *Clematis* 'Jackmanii Superba'

bears deep velvety-purple flowers – it just begs to scramble up through old roses of faded lavender and sultry purple, and 'Reine des Violettes' or 'Veilchenblau' would do beautifully.

Other climbing plants chosen to scent pergola walkways might include the honeysuckles, jasmines and mandevilla species. *Wisteria* is also an excellent choice, as the pendulous flowers hang down in a fragrant amethyst mist and the dense foliage encloses the walkway in shade. Its deciduous habit allows sunlight in during the cooler months and reveals the attractively curved and twisted form of the trunk and branches.

In very hot climates bougainvilleas, the trumpet vine *Campsis radicans* and passionfruit *Passiflora caerulea* make flamboyantly colourful screens. Ivy varieties provide evergreen interest and are hardy in areas where the going is tough.

The virginia creeper, *Vitis coignetiae*, bears large handsome leaves during the warmer months that turn into conflagrations of crimson, scarlet and russet in autumn. Plantings which include a variety of these climbers ensure that the pergola is clothed with plants offering year-round interest.

Bowers and arbours are variations on the pergola theme, but are smaller, more intimate, and usually incorporate a beautifully wrought or carved seat. They are semi-enclosed structures that support plants or have plants trained to enclose them. Arbours intended for romantic, rose-draped corners became popular in the eighteenth and nineteenth centuries, and similar bowers are (happily) finding their way back into secluded corners of our gardens today.

In the same era, the French and Italians designed elaborate arbour frames of wire or wrought iron, an idea eagerly adopted by the Victorians with their love of decorative structures. They also interpreted the idea in another way, designing topiary arbours. The dense foliage of evergreen hedging such as yew, pine or conifers was clipped into the shape of a small room surrounding a seat. Highly ornamental (and highly labour intensive!), they were often topped by the topiary figure of a bird or an animal.

We can use plants in much the same way today, creating bowers and arbours where no actual structural framework exists. A semi-circle of shrubs or small trees, preferably with attractive foliage and scented flowers, or a geometric grouping of conifers

A simple bridge folded into roses and old-fashioned perennials makes an attractive structure
in this small garden, encouraging the feet to travel across to find out what secrets lie on the other
side. The attractive silver tree in the background is the weeping silver pear,
Pyrus sacilifolia 'Pendula'.

or cypresses of upright form, may be arranged to provide an interesting and intimate corner in which to sit and relax.

The gazebo is perhaps the most popular decorative garden structure of all. The appeal of an attractively constructed miniature house set in a tranquil and secluded corner of the garden is universal. Usually constructed of wooden timbers and trellis panels, the gazebo is a permeable structure admitting light and air freely. The roof may be made of tin,

thatch, wooden shingles or slate tiles. The floor, depending on the sophistication of the design, may be of timber or a layer of bark or gravel.

The open structure of the gazebo distinguishes it from the summer house, which is usually a more permanent, enclosed structure, built of brick, stone or timber, with windows, door, floor and sturdy roof. The summer houses constructed for the great gardens of yesteryear were often elaborate and beautiful structures which are treasured today as architectural

A birdbath framed by honeysuckle encourages avian visitors and creates an attractive focal point in a cottage garden setting. The plants with handsome silver foliage to the right are *Celmisia semicordata* 'David Shackleton'.

gems. Designs for the gazebo of today generally come as DIY kitsets, and offer a wide variety of intriguing styles.

A gazebo may be used to form an important focal point in the landscape of the garden. It may punctuate or emphasise a certain area, become the axis or termination of a long vista, or draw the eye across an elegant sweep of lawn. Plantings on the gazebo are more restrained than those on the pergola – one does not want it to vanish beneath jungle-like climbers! Roses are traditional favourites for draping the gazebo, and climbers of restrained growth such as the apricot 'Buff Beauty', or beautifully-scented, creamy-white 'Sombreuil', are ideal.

The pergola, gazebo, arbour or bower fill the dual role of decorative and utilitarian purpose. As such, they have become an integral part of the garden scene, offering a cool retreat, an intimate scented corner where the heat of the day or the chill of the winter wind is tempered. They offer refuge from a sudden rainstorm; a garden room in which one can linger on summer evenings to watch the setting sun suffuse the garden with amber light; a place to study the shape, form and framework of the garden on a winter's day, undistracted by the multi-coloured floral tapestry of summer; a small oasis of quietude in which we may rest from the pace of modern living and watch the seasons turning.

Old brick walls, classic statuary and a profusion of old roses are decorative design features which are hands-down winners. They are combined here to superb effect. Stately irises frame a handsome fountainhead which spills water over a shell-like basin, bringing a sense of movement to an already enchanting scene.

Top left: An elegant summerhouse with a domed roof makes a highly ornamental structure in a formal garden of clipped box hedges and parterres of white roses.

Left: A handsome dovecote, fantail pigeons and old utensils used as decorative plant containers bring a lively sense of fun and movement to a rural cottage garden.

Top left: Old fence posts and weathered lengths of wood are combined to create a trellis support for roses, making a design feature which is both decorative and utilitarian.

Centre left: Coppery-pink rose 'Meg' with semi-double flowers bossed with maroon-red stamens adorns an attractive trellis fenceline.

Bottom left: Delicate golden-eyed *Abutilon vitifolium album* and stylish white-painted wooden archways combine to create an inviting arbour.

Opposite top: Gates and garden entrances give the visitor the first impression of what sort of garden is likely to lie beyond. From the outside, these attractive white gates allow a glimpse within; from the inside they create the focal point at the end of a long vista overhung with a spectacular spring canopy of pale pink *Malus* blossoms.

Opposite bottom left: An attractively patterned brick path passes under an archway hung with the old rose 'Albertine', forming a frame for the beautifully designed arbour on the opposite side of the tennis court.

Opposite bottom right: A long vine-covered arch-way makes an unusual and attractive structural feature, inviting the feet to travel along a shadowed pathway to the bridge at its end.

Top left: A trellis archway forms the support for the magnificent spectacle of *Clematis montana rubens* in full flower.

Centre left: A pergola decorated with the rose 'Bantry Bay' provides an attractive walkway linking house and outbuildings, and a sheltered place to sit and view the garden.

Bottom left: Folded into luxuriant plantings, this trellis gazebo with shingled roof tiles offers a secret retreat in a secluded corner of the garden.

Opposite: A simple trellis archway spans the gap between house and garage, softening a concrete path and providing both a support for plants and an attractive ornamental structure. The tall narrow aperture frames the knot garden within, inviting visitors to explore the scene for themselves. The pillar rose underplanted with the small daisy *Erigeron karvinskianus* is 'Handel'.

Acknowledgements

Thank you to the following gardeners for allowing us to reproduce the photographs of their gardens. The number and letter indicate the page reference and position of the photograph.

Bill Abercromby (Designer), Auckland 13
Clark & Kathleen Abbot, 'Greach', Whangarei 52, 86r, 150, 156t
Rebecca Amos, 'Te Mara', Kaukapakapa 155tr
Diana Anthony, 'Valley Homestead Gardens', Whangarei front cover, 29lb, 57b, 103, 109br, 110b, 128c, 136b, 137b, 141, 148, 149, 151, 155b, 159
Kate & Ray Archibald, Monks Bay, Christchurch 92
Tony Barnes & John Sole, 'Ngamamaku', Oakura 138t
Rod Barnett (Designer), Auckland 42, backcover tr
Barnsley House, Gloucestershire 124, 126l, 134b, back cover bl
Jacky Bentham, Takapuna 19
Maryan Bishop, 'The Roseraie', Remuera 153
Kathy and Peter Boardman, Remuera 77
Bob and Ellen Boot, Birkenhead 18l
Anne Bond, Mahoetahi, Waitara, Taranaki 37t, 158b
Ruve Booth, Howick 67b
Bourton House, Gloucestershire 75, 142
Keith Boyer, Opanuka Tropical Gardens, Henderson 51t
Peter Brady, Mt Eden 148tr
Yvonne & Gary Chunn, Parnell 65t
Sir Thomas & Lady Clark, 'Aotea', South Kaipara Heads 12
Sylvia Connelly, Dublin 152
Phil Cooke, Remuera 128
Jetta & Bruce Cornish, Parnell 155tl
Cross Hills, Kimbolton 115, 138b
Muriel & Bob Davison, 'Maple Glen', Wyndham 22, 95, 96l, 116
Denmans, Fontwell, West Sussex 129
Helen & Val Dillon, Ranelagh, Dublin 2,60t,61,78tb,84,154
Monica & Jim Dowell, Auckland 6, 15
Ethel Doyle, Mayfield, Canterbury 27b
Dunn, Cactus Garden, Sydney 46
Olive Dunn, Invercargill 126r,156b
Graham & Lee Dunster, Canterbury 53, 58t
Betty Erickson, Christchurch 69tr
Jane Evans, Nelson 68
Julia & Andrew Everest, Fendalton 5b, 39t, 69bl, 105, 112t, 146
Sue & Eric Faesenkloet, Takapuna 48
Christine Fernyhough, Auckland 9, 79b
Diana Firth, Cox's Creek, Auckland 16
Susan Firth, Ponsonby 70l, 145l, 4t
Barry Gadsby, Edgeware, Christchurch 5t, 40c
Gethsemene Gardens, Sumner 25, 29rb, 158t, back cover bl
Geraldine & Rob Gillies, Mt Eden 21, 24
'Glenfalloch Gardens', Dunedin 116, 118, 119
Susanna Grace, 'Rathmoy', Hunterville 128tr
Shirley & Ian Greenhill, Stratford, Taranaki 131
Denis Greville, Christchurch 62
Trish & John Gribben, Parnell 88b
Sara & Paul Grigg, Surrey Hills, South Canterbury 121t
Jo & Gonda La Grouw, 'Hillgonda', Rotorua 59b, 96r, 117
Hadspen House, Somerset 104
Geoffrey Haughey & Richard Cadness, 'Westridge', Titirangi 7, 114
Annie Heywood, Merivale 79t, 156c, 158c
Ilam Gardens, Christchurch 119
Joan & Keith Innes, 'Elgin', Christchurch 77tr
Ann & Alan Izard, 'Wilsons Mill', Ohoka, Canterbury 73
Annette & Noel Johnson, Taipairi Point, Whenuapai 39b, 112c, 132, 148bl
Collen & Ray Jones, Whenuapai 4b
Martin Keay (Designer), Auckland 157t
Barbara Kerr, Fendalton 120br
Debbie Kerr, Christchurch 122
Jo & Patrick Kerr, Christchurch 109t
Kiftsgate Court, Gloucestershire 107t
Arno King (Designer), Campbells Bay, Auckland 45, 50
Elga & Vilnis Lagzdins, Shirley 36, 91
Judy & Tony Laity, 'Cottonwood', Panmure 38tr, 38bl
Lau Waiman, Auckland 134t

Pat & Selwyn Lawrence, Hunterville 30, 31
Jim & Pat Lawson, Pakuranga 18b
Suzanne & David Lee, 'Quailscroft', Whitford 121b
Vana Leeming, Harewood 37b, 70b, 145r
Beverley & Malcolm McConnell, 'Ayrlies', Whitford 133, 138r and back cover tl
Doris & Kim McFarlane, Gore Bay, Canterbury 18t
Pam & Max McMasters, Halswell, Canterbury 57t, 60b
Marnie Mackesy, Remuera 69bl
Joanna & Peter Masfen, Auckland 83
Adie & Matt McLellan, Kelburn 71
Sally & Paul Masson, New Plymouth 135bl
Gwyn Masters, 'Aramaunga', Stratford 119, 4c
Barbara & Douglas Meyers, Auckland 1, 76, 85, 89b, 106
Joan & Peter Money, Northcote 49b
Diana & Colin Monro, Mt Pleasant, Christchurch 108t
Betty & Charles Moore, 'Westwood', Waititi, Otago 99r, 120t
Jean Morrison, Karori 70tr
Marion Morris, Fendalton 69tl, 87b
Diana & Colin Monro, Mt Pleasant, Christchurch 108t
Liz Morrow, Glendowie 17t
Alison & Sam Morton, Devonport 135tr
Mottisfont Abbey Gardens, Hampshire 87t
Mount Stewart, Newtownards, Northern Ireland 40b, 100c, 130
Allie & Ivan Nagel, Remuera, Gary Boyle (Designer) 135tr
Elizabeth & Stuart Nicholls, Fendalton 102
'Ohinetahi', Governors Bay, Canterbury 72, 77tl, 111b, 136t, 147b
Jan & Brian Oldham, Meadowbank 120bl
Old Rectory, Sudborough, Northamptonshire 125, 128b
Elizabeth & Peter Ormond, Havelock North 26
Vivien & Daniel Papich, 'Bellevue', Langs Beach 10, 20, 29tr, 40t, 82, 88t, 89b, 93, 98, 110t, 148tl, 149
Anthony Paul & Hannah Peschar, Sculpture Garden, Ockley, Surrey 34, 101
Suzy & Richard Paynter, Fendalton 109bl, 147tr, 157bl
Helen Phare & Rodney Kirk-Smith, Ponsonby 127r
Joan & Paul Pollock, 'Highgate', Gisborne 99bl
Powis Castle, Powys, Wales 157br
Raupara Watergardens, Tapu, Coromandel 49t
Nan & Wynne Raymond, 'Ethridge Gardens', Timaru 3, 56, 86l, 90
Jim Reynolds, Butterstream, Meath, Ireland 74, 80, 81, 100b, 125
Elizabeth & Graeme Robertson, 'Crosshills', Otorohanga 54
Diana & Andrew Robertson, Fendalton 107b,108b
Rosemoore Gardens, Devon 111t
Gay & John Rutherford, 'Gola Peak', Hawarden, Canterbury 27t
A. Ryan, Whangarei 47
Liz & Warren Scott, Ruapuna, Ashburton 35, 121c
Noel Scotting, Whitford 43, 51
Elspeth & Graham Shannon, Cheltenham, Manawatu 28
Ted Smythe (Designer), Auckland 137t
Diana Spencer, Ramaroa, Te Kuiti 99t
Terry Stringer, Parnell 66
Liz & David Sumpter, 'Rangimarie', Waitati, Otago 38tl
Jacqui & Alistair Sutherland, 'Whangaimoana', Wairarapa 55
Gillian Templeton, Forrest Hill, North Shore City 8
Denis & Ruth Thom, Wellington 135br
'Titoki Point', Gordon & Annette Collier, Taihape 41, 58, 97t
Barbara & Ric Toogood, 'Reviresco', Havelock North 112b
Alan & Catherine Trott, Ashburton 100t, 140
Suzanne Turley, Orakei, Auckland 63
Jeannie & Andrew Van der Puten, Grey Lynn 67
Sarah & John Vickers, Woodleigh Farm, Marton 79c
'Waimanu', Auckland 97b
Robert Watson (Designer), Christchurch 94
John & Barbara Whitehead, Taunahunga Tropical Gardens, Matakana 33, 44
Kath & Noel Widdowson, 'The Nugget', South Otago 114
Daphne & Hugh Wilson, Gore Bay, Canterbury 11, 15
Juliet & Peter Worsp, Christchurch 64
Pam Wratten, 'Lavender Patch', Lower Moutere, Nelson 23, 32, 113
Penny Zino, 'Flaxmere', Harwarden 59t, 59c, 139